SAY-IT-FAITH

To Charles Pa Henson
You have great faith, but it
can still grow. I trust you
can move mountain & serve God.

Elmer Towns
1 Thess 5:24

Say-It-Faith

ELMER L. TOWNS

 Tyndale House Publishers, Inc., Wheaton, Illinois

First printing, March 1983

Library of Congress Catalog Card Number 82-73454
ISBN 0-8423-5825-0
Copyright © 1983 by Elmer L. Towns
All rights reserved
Printed in the United States of America

CONTENTS

Introduction 7
1 Say-It-Faith 11
2 Natural Faith and Biblical Faith 27
3 Saving Faith 35
4 Living by Faith 55
5 Justification by Faith 75
6 Indwelling Faith 83
7 The Gift of Faith 95
8 The Statement of Faith 103
9 How to Grow Faith 111
10 Kept by Faith 119
11 Overcoming the Factors That Destroy Faith 127
Conclusion 139
Footnotes 141
Bibliography 143

INTRODUCTION

Many years ago I added the word "Faith" to the top of my prayer list and prayed fervently for God to give me faith because I wanted to be a man of faith. But my prayers were not answered because that is not the way God works. God does not fill up anyone with faith as someone might fill up an empty glass.

First, to develop faith we must saturate ourselves with the Word of God because "faith cometh by hearing and hearing by the word of God" (Romans 10:17). To get faith we must study carefully the Scriptures. Second, faith grows through experiences, both positive ones that build us up and negative ones that teach us what not to do. This is called "the trial of your faith" (1 Peter 1:7). In the third place, our faith cannot be separated from our service to God. The Lord does not give us faith so that we might cherish it like a souvenir on a coffee table. Faith grows as it is used in winning souls or trusting God for money.

God did not give me faith as someone gives a birthday gift, but God did motivate me to study the topic of faith in the Scriptures. I wanted to know every shade of meaning concerning faith. In my study I found at least six types of New Testament faith.

Actually, this book grew out of another. I began writing a chapter on faith for a theology textbook. Everything I wrote was unsatisfactory, so I continued studying and writing page after page. I began reading every book I could find written on faith. Almost every book on faith that I read discussed the content of faith, which refers to doctrinal content. Very few books offer help in developing stronger faith in God, to move mountains. I found some books on subjective faith, but they dealt mostly with the Christian life in general, not specifically on faith. Since I could not find the book I wanted, I decided to write it.

I have interviewed many of the pastors who have built the largest churches in the world. I consider them to be men of faith so I wrote and asked them for their articles, sermons, or their insights on faith. These men had won thousands of souls to Christ, and raised countless millions of dollars by faith. I listened to tapes of their sermons and read their articles. I remembered what they told me when I interviewed them. They usually said publicly what they were going to do for God. Their public statement was not egotistical bragging. I sensed confidence in their voices when they said what they were going to do. Their confidence seemed born of the Spirit of God. This is when I decided to call this book *Say-It-Faith*. Faith is reflective of God who "calleth those things which be not as though they were" (Romans 4:17).

When the book was almost finished, I began preaching a sermon on the topic "Say-It-Faith." When I first preached it at prayer meeting for Thomas Road Baptist Church, I told one of the pastors that I was asking God for one hundred persons to come forward during the invitation to dedicate their lives to Christ. I felt a sermon on faith must reflect faith. Usually only five or six responded to the invitation on Wednesday evenings. However that evening people kept responding. The congregation sang stanza after stanza of an invitation hymn. After the meeting I asked Dr. Sumner Wemp, Vice President of Spiritual Affairs at Liberty Baptist College, how many came forward. He said over a hundred. When I asked Rev. Ed Dobson, Dean of Students, he said over two hundred. Every time I preached this sermon in a different church, the response was evident; God was using the message of Say-It-Faith.

In this book, *Say-It-Faith* is capitalized because it is a title, describing the highest expression of faith. Also, Say-It-Faith is hyphenated because *say* and *it* are used to describe the noun *faith*.

This book is written that you might be "full of faith" (Acts 6:5, 11:24) to the praise, honor, and glory of Jesus Christ.

Elmer L. Towns
Lynchburg, Virginia

ONE
SAY-IT-FAITH

Without argument or persuasion, I want you to say what you will do to meet a world's need, and to help to carry on his gigantic struggle. William Booth, Salvation Army

Say-It-Faith means we should say what we want God to do for us so he will do it. "For verily I say unto you, That whosoever shall say unto this mountain, Be thou removed, and be thou cast into the sea; and shall not doubt in his heart, but shall believe that those things which he saith shall come to pass; he shall have whatsoever he saith" (Mark 11:23).

Three times in this verse Jesus told his disciples to "say" what they wanted from God. But not every person who says what he wants gets it. Why? Perhaps he has not completely followed God's formula for Say-It-Faith. First, he must say what he wants. Second, he must not doubt what he is doing. Third, he must believe that he will get his answer. Fourth, he must ask in prayer and God will move the mountain out of his life.

Faith takes many forms, but perhaps the greatest kind is evidenced by a confidence in God so deep that one not only knows he will get the thing for which he trusts, but he publicly tells others that he expects to do so. This is called Say-It-Faith, which involves saying what one wants God to do before he does it. Say-It-Faith is taught by Jesus when he commanded his disciples, "Have faith in God. For verily I say unto you, That whosoever shall *say* unto this mountain, Be thou removed, and be thou cast into the sea; and shall not doubt in his heart, but shall believe that those things which he *saith* shall come to pass; he shall have whatsoever he saith" (Mark 11:22, 23; italics added).

Jerry Falwell has practiced Say-It-Faith but never thought of it in those terms until I preached a sermon in Thomas Road Baptist Church from this text, entitled "Say-It-Faith." In January 1977, Liberty Baptist College faced the prospect of no buildings for the fall. The classes had been meeting in an unused public high school in the city and in other rented facilities throughout Lynchburg. The school board advised the college that they were tearing down the old high school. Jerry Falwell announced that there was a two million dollar debt and that there was no way to borrow the money to build on Liberty Mountain. Besides that, no other rental building could be found in Lynchburg for the college. Obviously, Jerry Falwell and Liberty Baptist College faced an overwhelming obstacle.

Jesus instructed his disciples to ". . . say unto this mountain, Be thou removed." Since the word "mountain" meant "obstacle," Falwell needed faith to overcome his problem. The entire student body went up on Liberty Mountain and stood in eight inches of snow for a telecast. Over 1200 students prayed and sang, "I Want That Mountain." Jerry Falwell told the television audience that he needed two million dollars in the next few months to pay off the indebtedness so they could build. The students prayed during the television broadcast and God began touching hearts all over America. Within two months the money came in and immediately the bulldozers moved onto Liberty Mountain. Two classroom buildings were ready for the students when they arrived on campus in September.

Jerry Falwell had practiced Say-It-Faith by first announcing what he wanted. Secondly, he did not doubt that God would provide, since he was doing God's will. And, third, he believed God for the things that he requested.

But that was not a random exercise of Say-It-Faith. Jerry Falwell has made faith a daily practice. As a matter of fact, the theme song of the radio portion of the Old-Time Gospel Hour is "We've Come This Far by Faith."

When I first met Jerry Falwell, he was driving to television rallies in churches around the state of Virginia. One night I went with him up in the Blue Ridge Mountains, to speak to an audience of approximately 300 people. Before the service Falwell asked me how many "Doorkeepers" we would enlist that evening. A Doorkeeper was a person who promised to send one dollar a month to keep the Old-Time Gospel Hour on the air. I looked over the audience and thought about fifty people might sign up. Jerry said, "No, I'm trusting God for a hundred." After the program, when people raised their hands to be Doorkeepers, over one hundred people responded.

On another occasion, as Sunday school superintendent of the Thomas Road Sunday school, I met with the staff and Jerry Falwell to set a goal for Harvest Day 1971. To our knowledge, no Sunday school had ever broken 10,000 in attendance. On a previous occasion I had said that 10,000 was a reachable goal, but I did not have faith to think that our Sunday school could do it. At the time attendance averaged about 4,300.

At the staff meeting we did not arrive at a goal. That evening Jerry Falwell stood before the prayer meeting and announced, "I feel that God would have us accept the challenge of 10,000 in Sunday school."

As I sat on the platform, my first reaction was unbelief

and fear of embarrassment. I was afraid of what people would think about my reputation if we did not reach a goal of 10,000 people. I had written books on Sunday school, but obviously I was not an authority on faith. During that campaign I began to learn the lesson of Say-It-Faith.

We did not sit back and wait for God to bring them in. We organized the entire Sunday school for work. First we asked 107 ladies each to take a page of the phone book and phone everyone in the city and invite them to attend Sunday school. An invitation to the Sunday school was posted on twelve billboards along the major highways into Lynchburg. Over 5,000 posters and handbills were distributed throughout the city, the teenagers put them under the windshield wipers of every car in parking lots. Sixty radio announcements were made on every radio station, inviting visitors to Sunday school. Three letters were mailed to every home in the area, inviting the residents to attend Sunday school. In addition to the other advertisements, over 200 people came out Saturday morning to go to every home in the city to invite people to Sunday school. Harvest Day brought *10,187* to Sunday school. That great victory came by faith. Faith had conceived the goal, and faith had motivated the people to work. Faith had touched the heart of God so that he was moved by a pastor and people who *said* what they wanted *before* the victory was won.

Jerry Falwell announces publicly what he believes God will do. It is common practice among pastors to announce Sunday school goals. They have prayed for evangelistic outreach to the community, then they have organized the workers to visit the lost. In an act of faith, they have "said it" so that God will honor their faith and give them the victory.

Perhaps the greatest victory of Say-It-Faith happened in the fall of 1978. That year Liberty Baptist College had built sixteen dormitories on Liberty Mountain by faith. An indebtedness of five million dollars had accumulated. This time over 2,000 students gathered for a television rally, near the spot where they had prayed eighteen months earlier. Dr. Falwell told the television audience that the dormitories had to be built because so many students had applied to the college. He felt God had led him not to turn down any student who wanted to come to Liberty. Therefore, God had provided for them.

The students gathered on a grassy knoll and once again sang "I Want That Mountain." Jerry looked into the camera and said by faith that he wanted the people to help him pay for these buildings—five million dollars. Then all the students knelt in small groups across Liberty Mountain. They asked God for the five million dollars. Later, when I saw the telecast, I realized that the camera had caught me praying. I told God, "I do not have faith for five million dollars, but I want faith. Nevertheless, I do ask for five million dollars." Then I went on to pray, "Please give me faith to believe you for great victories." Finally, I prayed like the father of the demon-possessed boy in the Scriptures, "Lord, help thou my unbelief."

After the telecast was shown and all the money was counted, over seven million dollars was received in response to the faith of Jerry Falwell. I interviewed his wife, Macel, for a story in the *Journal Champion* newspaper. I asked her if she felt that at any time Jerry Falwell had wavered in his faith? She responded, "I personally did not have the faith that Jerry had." She confessed that five million was a big goal. Finally she said, "I don't think Jerry had the slightest doubt at any time that the five million dollars would come in."

During the summer of 1961, I became president of Winnipeg Bible College in Canada. The school had an oppressive debt and there was no money to pay salaries. Everyone looked to me as the spiritual leader of the college. Beside the debt, the school had a no-solicitation policy. Technically it was termed "full-information without solicitation."

On at least two occasions I prayed all night that God

would send in the money. Even though I was young at the time, twenty-seven years old, age makes no difference in faith. My problem was that I did not understand the biblical principles of Say-It-Faith.

First, I did not announce to the faculty, board members, or the student body, that we were going to pray the money in. In essence I did not "Say unto the mountain, Be thou removed." A second problem was that I did not specify a certain amount of money. I just prayed in general for money. God honors all kinds of prayers, and some money did come in. But the victorious answer that I wanted was not realized. I grew a little in my faith, but I did not grow in a great way, because I had not trusted God for a great answer to prayer.

We do not get Say-It-Faith just by announcing a goal ahead of time. Many Sunday schools have announced a goal, but have fallen short. Many times a pastor has announced a financial need, but the money did not come in. There are biblical factors necessary for Say-It-Faith. First, we must not doubt in our hearts. Faith comes from God, and only God can give inner confidence to trust him for miracles. Second, the person must believe that "whatsoever he saith" shall come to pass.

Three Korean girls were attending a Christian camp somewhere in Korea. The stream that separated the camp from the small nearby town had flooded. The three girls needed to get to the town, but could not cross the flooded creek. They knew the Bible story of Peter walking on water. The three girls knelt and asked God to help them walk on water. Then as a seal of their confidence, they told their friends they were going to walk on the water. They felt that they must demonstrate their faith because they had asked God for a miracle. When the floods subsided, all three bodies were found washed ashore downstream.

This story is a sad commentary of people who have misguided faith. But the worst results came when the newspapers printed the complete story on the front page, in essence, mocking Christianity. To the Orientals who are so concerned about "saving face," the church was humiliated in the eyes of the unsaved. Therefore, it is imperative that when we exercise Say-It-Faith, we make sure our faith is born from above.

I taught a summer school class at Baptist University of America, Atlanta, Georgia, a few years ago. As students are inclined to do, a young boy tried to flirt with a young girl. Over a period of two or three days, I noticed his pursuits of her affections got more intense. He sat next to her, talked with her, but she was obviously trying to ignore him. After class one day, I found out that the girl in question had recently sneaked off to Alabama and married another college student, but not the boy who was flirting with her. The couple had not told anyone. As a matter of fact, their mothers and fathers did not know they were married either.

When I learned they were married, I wondered how I could help them with their problem. Just about that time, the young boy who flirted with the girl walked into my office. He was very bold, and felt he ought to announce his intentions. He said, "I am going to marry that girl, even though she doesn't like me now." He went on to describe how he could woo her and make her like him. Finally he said, "I feel it is the will of God for me to marry a nice, wholesome girl, and she is the one." I wanted to tell him how wrong he was about the will of God, but I could not say anything because we had not yet informed the parents.

Many people express their faith like that young boy—they get their confident feelings mixed up with their faith. They have convinced themselves that *what they want* is the will of God; therefore, by faith, they "say it." But the answers do not come and they grow disillusioned. Say-It-Faith is a biblical principle but, like all principles, it can be violated by human abuse.

Say-It-Faith is also called "the word of faith" (Romans 10:8). When Paul uses the phrase "the word of faith," he is pointing to our spoken words of faith. There are two Greek words for "word." The first, *logos*, means "a word as the expression of an inner thought." The other is *rhema*, which means "word in the outward form as a part of speech."

When Paul said, "the word is nigh thee, even in thy mouth, and in thy heart: that is, the word of faith, which we preach" (Romans 10:8), he is using the term *rhema*. The faith of our heart is to be spoken by the mouth.

Later, when Paul said, "So then faith cometh by hearing, and hearing by the word of God" (Romans 10:17), the "word" of God is *rhema*, which means that people get saved by the spoken Word of God as they listen to a sermon or as a soul-winner testifies to them. The soul-winners that are most effective are those who quote the written Word, the Bible, and are motivated by the spoken word (*rhema*) of faith. They know God will work in the hearts of those who are lost. The very fact that they began testifying to a lost person is their Say-It-Faith. Say-It-Faith must always be in agreement with the principles of the written Word of God. But Say-It-Faith goes further; it must be enlightened by the spoken Word of God. Since the Word of God gives confidence, those who base their ministry upon it will minister in confidence.

Say-It-Faith involves the total commitment of the person to a task. That person has confidence that God will do what he says. The old farmer was wrong when he said that "Faith is believing what ain't so." Faith is never a leap into the dark. Rather, faith is a leap into the light. When we move by faith, we know where we are stepping, because we are walking in the light of the Word of God.

Several years ago, a student at Liberty Bible Institute needed $190 to pay for his rent and groceries. He decided to exercise faith. He had fifty dollars in the checking account, but that was only half enough to pay for his rent, and there was no money to pay for groceries. He made a commitment to God, so he wrote a check for fifty dollars and put it in the offering plate. That left him nothing, but he believed God would supply his need. When he got home, he told his wife what he had done. His landlord was a member of Thomas Road Baptist Church. Since the student thought his landlord might give him the month's rent free if he knew what he had done, they told no one what they did, since they had made a total commitment in faith.

The student was certain that God would answer his prayer, and determined that the answer would not come through the sympathy of his friends. Before the end of the week, he received a check for $190 in the mail from the last company where he had worked. He had already received his severance pay and did not expect any more. This check was the balance of his retirement pay and the company was simply clearing its account, but God was moving by faith to supply the young man's needs.

Say-It-Faith is not human faith directed toward God. Say-It-Faith is a supernatural ability of God whereby he plants in the human heart the gift to trust him for marvelous results in Christian service. The Bible teaches that Say-It-Faith grows from weak faith into strong faith. When Jerry Falwell first began his ministry, he could only trust God for fifty dollars for supplies. That amount was needed so the men of the church could build an extension to an old bottling plant, a small concrete building approximately thirty-by-sixty-feet, where the church was started. There was no space for Sunday school, so evenings and Saturdays the laymen constructed a one-room addition. Even as God was providing fifty dollars for those supplies, the children held class on a dirt floor. As Jerry Falwell learned to trust God for smaller things, God increased his faith. Today, he can trust God for a million dollars a day to keep the total ministry going.

The faith of Abraham is described as "not weak"

(Romans 4:19). He was approaching one hundred years of age and Sarah, age ninety, was past the time of having children. Though Abraham had failed in his faith on other occasions, in this promise, Abraham staggered not. The Bible says, "He was strong in faith" (Romans 4:20). It is possible for a person to grow from "weak faith" to "strong faith." Evidently God gave Abraham occasions to trust him to enable Abraham to be led out of Ur and later out of Haran by faith.

Just as a church grows from victory to victory, so our faith may grow by "saying the victory" and seeing it accomplished. No man becomes the heavyweight champion of the world unless he is victorious over his opponents. He too must go from victory to victory to get the ultimate prize.

To have Say-It-Faith, we must reflect the Lord God in whose image we are created. Concerning God, it is said he "calleth those things which be not as though they were" (Romans 4:17). So if we want to grow in faith, we must call those things which are not as though they were. Abraham had faith when circumstances were discouraging, "who against hope believed in hope" (Romans 4:18).

To have Say-It-Faith, we must have explicit confidence in the promises of God written in the Scriptures. Perhaps one of the best biblical definitions of faith is, "And being fully persuaded that, what he had promised, he was able also to perform" (Romans 4:21). Lest we think that the promises of God were only for Abraham, David, or other men of God in the Old Testament, Paul stated that faith is available "for us also" (Romans 4:24).

There are many ways to express Say-It-Faith. First, we say it by writing what we want on a prayer list. The act of writing is an expression of our expectations. God, who knows all things, sees our penned prayer requests. But, more than the words, he honors the faith behind the request (John 14:14; Matthew 7:7, 8). Hence, a prayer list is an expression of Say-It-Faith.

A second way to express Say-It-Faith is orally, with a prayer partner. As we tell someone our prayer request, we make a declaration of faith that we look to God and expect his help. Then, in prayer, we articulate in words what we want God to do. The agreement together is Say-It-Faith. Jesus said that, "If two of you shall agree on earth as touching any thing that they shall ask, it shall be done for them of my Father which is in heaven" (Matthew 18:19).

A third expression of Say-It-Faith is to give a testimony or to request prayer in church. R. C. Worley, a founding member of Thomas Road Baptist Church, frequently has the church pray for him. There may be many other reasons why he is one of the most effective soul-winners in the church, but his faith to request prayer is one of the reasons. It takes an act of faith to ask somebody else to pray for our requests. We may ask people to pray for an unsaved loved one, or to help our Sunday school class, or to heal a sick person, or to supply finances. One of the reasons why the power of God is so evident at the services at Thomas Road Baptist Church is that many people constantly ask for prayer. In every service, the ushers are continually handing prayer request cards to Dr. Jerry Falwell. Cards are provided in the pew racks marked "prayer request." Several times during a service an usher will collect the cards and bring them to Dr. Falwell. As he stands to begin the service with prayer, two or three cards may be handed to him. He will read the requests and ask the audience to pray with him. The same procedure is repeated when he stands to take the offering. Even when the benediction is given at the end of the service, personal requests for prayer are added. Hence, the congregation as a whole is exercising Say-It-Faith.

Another way of exercising Say-It-Faith is to set an attendance or a financial goal. Many times Sunday school campaigns have an attendance goal. At other times, there is a financial goal, or a goal for the building fund.

Sometimes a missionary will share his financial need with the congregation. In essence, he is exercising Say-It-Faith by trusting God and asking for support to go to the mission field.

A fifth way of exercising Say-It-Faith is to pray at the church altar. For many years those of the Wesleyan tradition have invited people to come and pray at the altar at the front of the sanctuary. Baptists have traditionally invited only lost people to come forward to be saved. In recent years, the Baptists have installed church altars and have taught their people to use the altar as a place to get answers to prayer. Whereas many Christians may be reluctant to kneel at an altar during a church service, the public testimony of a person's need may prove the credibility of his faith. Perhaps the reluctance to ask for prayer, even to publicly confess that they have a need, is lack of faith. At the Thomas Road Baptist Church the people use the stairs leading to the pulpit area as an altar for prayer. Many times a student will ask a pastor to pray with him concerning money or for an unsaved relative. Sometimes a person will ask prayer concerning a habit over which he wants victory. Recently a student came to pray for his roommate. Finally, he confessed that he was the cause of the problem, not his roommate. In his confession he said he was the one who always got angry. Sometimes Say-It-Faith provides a strong motivation by pointing the finger back into the person's own heart, revealing his unbelief and sin.

Say-It-Faith is not an instant solution to all our problems, but it comes as a result of a dedicated life and knowledge of the Word of God. Actually, Say-It-Faith is only one expression of faith, perhaps the hardest to achieve in the Christian life. If we do not have the ability to *say* what we want and *receive* it, then we should examine ourselves. There are six areas of faith, each with different results in our lives. As we compare our faith to each of the six areas, if we cannot say to a mountain/

problem, "Be thou removed," then we may be lacking in one of these areas.

Faith is found in six different settings, but each one has the similar property, such as trusting God, leaning on God, or relying on him completely. All six types of faith, which we will discuss in subsequent chapters, are reflections of natural faith, which involve repudiation of self-trust and complete reliance on God. But each of the six types of faith is manifested in a different way and accomplishes a different result. Some Christians have not *walked by faith,* even though they are *saved by faith.* Maybe they have wrongly applied the laws of faith after their conversion. Perhaps they have been searching for an *active faith* to help them daily, but they wrongly understand *imputed faith* which applies only to their perfection in heaven.

The first expression is *saving faith.* In Greek, the noun *pistis,* "faith," is translated into action by the *pisteuo,* "I believe." When the Philippian jailer cried out, "What must I do to be saved?" he was commanded, "Believe on the Lord Jesus Christ and thou shalt be saved" (Acts 16:31). When the sinner expresses the active verb of belief, the observer describes conversion by a noun, "He has *faith.*"

The second is *sanctifying faith.* Paul explained this: "We walk by faith, not by sight" (2 Corinthians 5:7). When a Christian is living by faith, he is trusting God for everything. He puts his faith in God for victory over sin, for joy, for fruit, wisdom, illumination into the Word, and for God's leading in his daily life. Beyond these spiritual qualities, those who walk by faith must trust God for physical protection, food, clothing, and a roof over their heads.

The third is *imputed faith,* which happens in heaven and is nonexperiential for us. Paul taught the doctrine of justification by faith, whereby God declares that a sinner becomes righteous by faith. It is not a matter of how much faith a person has. When he trusts God he is declared righteous before God.

Some have confused justification by faith with sanctifying faith. They feel that since they are perfect in heaven, they have no further obligation on earth. They give themselves over to the lust of the flesh, they live selfish lives, and no longer strive against sin. However, every Christian must grow daily by faith. Faith can grow because the Bible teaches that some are "weak in faith" while others are "strong in faith." Sanctifying faith is a growing faith.

The fourth kind is *indwelling faith*. This faith lives within us, but it does not belong to us. It is the faith of Jesus Christ who indwells the believer. The faith of Jesus Christ is perfect and does not need to grow. It is the faith that overcomes the world. When Christ comes to dwell in a believer, he makes available his faith to him. Just as Jesus Christ never sinned, so he can help the believer overcome sin. Just as Jesus Christ always did the will of the Father, so he helps the believer do the perfect will of God. Just as Jesus Christ said, "I do always those things that please thee," so the believer can have perfect fellowship with the Father.

The fifth kind of faith is the *gift of faith*. Among the many and varied gifts of the Holy Spirit, God supernaturally gives us the ability to serve him by exercising faith (Romans 12:7). This is more than the gift of salvation. This is called a "serving gift" or an ability whereby a person serves God by exercising faith. Not everyone has all of the gifts, so not everyone has the gift of faith. Paul explained that the gifts differ: "Having then gifts differing according to the grace that is given to us" (Romans 12:6). God has given some the gift of faith to enable them effectively to carry out their ministry in a greater way.

George Mueller had great answers to prayer; perhaps his secret was the gift of faith—the ability to trust God to provide the needs of the orphanage in Bristol, England. Once the dining hall was empty and over 2,000 hungry orphans waited for dinner. Mueller exercised faith and thanked God for the meal. Then the driver of a broken wagon knocked at the door to tell he had a wagon full of bread that could not be delivered. Mueller had announced to approximately 2,000 orphans what he expected God to supply; that was Say-It-Faith, which is a gift from God.

If God has given us the gift of faith, we need to exercise it faithfully in keeping with well-balanced Christianity. Paul said, "Though I have all faith, so that I could remove mountains, and have not charity, I am nothing" (1 Corinthians 13:2).

The Bible teaches that the proper use of our gifts increases the effectiveness and usefulness of the gifts (Matthew 25:14-36). It also teaches that we can desire and pray for more gifts (1 Corinthians 12:31). Therefore, we can have more faith to trust God for bigger things than we have now. If we are faithful in small things, God will give us more faith.

The sixth type of faith is the doctrinal *statement of faith*. Whenever the article *the* is used with faith, it usually refers to doctrine. Doctrinal faith is not subjective, so it cannot grow. It never changes. Doctrinal faith is the written expression of God himself. It is immutable, eternal, and the expression of truth.

This book examines the six types of faith so every Christian can grow to trust God for greater answers to prayer. Other kinds of faith mentioned in this book, such as dead faith, natural faith, and rational faith are not biblical faith. These are examined to help us see God's complete picture of trusting him.

Finally, the last section of this book deals with the practical aspects of faith. How to grow faith, what happens when God brings trials to increase our faith, and the practical applications of faith.

TWO
NATURAL FAITH
AND BIBLICAL FAITH

Faith consists, not in ignorance, but in knowledge, and that, not only of God, but also of the divine will.
John Calvin

Not everyone has Say-It-Faith, but everyone who has sat in a chair or driven a car has experienced faith—natural faith. Faith is one of the attributes of humanity. Everyone exercises faith. Some are more trusting than others, while others have lost their trusting nature for one reason or another. Natural faith will not save anyone, the cynic nor those who are naturally trusting. "For by grace are ye saved through faith; and that not of yourselves: it is the gift of God: Not of works, lest any man should boast" (Ephesians 2:8, 9).

To be saved a person must have biblical faith, which is given by God. Biblical faith enables a person to believe in God and to build a life of faith in God.

Some illustrations of faith, similar to New Testament faith, appear in everyday life and describe it to us. But such faith is not the same as biblical faith, which is the gift of God (Ephesians 2:8, 9). These only illustrate faith, only God can create faith.

An evangelist wanted to teach his son something about faith. He placed him on the table and backed up three or four feet, then told the little fellow, "Jump."

The little boy shook his head. "Papa, I'm afraid."

"Jump and I'll catch you," the evangelist told his son. "Trust me."

The little fellow was ready to jump, but looked down at the floor and cried, "I'm afraid!"

"Didn't I tell you I would catch you, son?" the evangelist said. "Will Papa deceive you?"

The boy shook his head. He wanted to believe his father but was having a hard time doing it. So the father encouraged him, "Look me right in the eye and jump: I will catch you."

The little fellow got ready to jump for a third time and again froze. "I'm afraid."

The promise of the father was not enough, nor was the fact that he stared into his father's eyes. The boy was afraid to do what he had never done before. So the father asked, "Have I ever hurt you?"

"No."

"Will you obey me?"

"Yes."

"Now jump!" the father held out his arms.

The little boy leaped into his father's arms. When his father caught him they both laughed and hugged each other. The boy had learned the natural lesson of faith. Immediately the little boy said, "Let me jump again."

His father put him back on the table and he jumped again and again. The father could step back a few steps and still the boy would jump. The little boy had learned to trust his father.

The Scriptures describe such confidence. "He that hath received his testimony hath set to his seal that God is true" (John 3:33). Those who have learned to trust in God have put their seal upon the truthfulness of God. Unbelief says, "I can't," while faith says, "I will."

Faith can be described as receiving a gift. If one were in a prison cell and the jailor brought him a pardon, he would have to receive it to get out of prison. The pardon would be valid because it was signed by the governor, but it would not become effective until the person received it and walked out of the cell. Saving faith is simply receiving God's pardon for sin, accomplished by Christ on the cross. Forgiveness, like all spiritual reality, cannot be given unless it is taken. Therefore, faith is receiving God's forgiveness.

Faith can be described as entering a door. A passenger had a deep fear of flying on an airplane. He talked to his friends and read everything he could find about flying, but could not force himself to board an airplane. Finally he went to see a psychiatrist. The psychiatrist arranged with the airline company for the man to tour a plane that was parked on the ground. The passenger had no difficulty entering the plane because he knew it was not going to take off. Yet, after purchasing a ticket he froze at the cabin door. He could not enter the plane. No matter how hard he tried to convince himself, it was futile. He could not trust the airplane because of fear.

Genuine faith is resting in the work of Christ. Some have said that faith is like sitting in a chair. When sitting down, one puts all of his trust in the chair. He rests in the strength of the chair. If he suspends himself above the chair, and keeps all of the weight on his legs, he has not completely rested on the chair. He has not trusted the chair. Faith means letting go. It is complete rest in the chair, knowing it will hold him up. In the same way, when one puts faith in Jesus Christ he leans on him for everything.

A hiker hitched a ride on a wagon, yet when he climbed aboard he kept his pack on his back. The driver of the wagon told him, "Put down your pack and rest awhile." The hiker shook his head, explaining that he was grateful for the ride and did not want to put extra weight on the mule pulling the wagon. In the same way, some people come to salvation but will not rest their entire sin-burden on Jesus Christ.

Faith can be compared to turning on a light switch. The result of faith, as exercised in throwing the switch, was that once the switch was turned on the light illuminated the room. The effectiveness of faith was not in the act of turning on the switch, but in the fact that the switch was connected by wire to a generating plant outside the home.

Some have mistakenly put their faith in outward things, such as singing hymns, reading the Bible, or praying. When they turn on the switch, the light of faith does not go on. They may have faith in their faith, or faith in their good works, but the way to get results is to have faith in God.

A missionary told of a national who sneaked into his house and stole the light switch, wire, and light bulb. He ran back into the jungle and displayed it to his tribe. Attaching the switch to his grass hut and hanging the light bulb from the ceiling, he flipped the switch and nothing happened. The native had faith in the switch, as many have faith in good works. They thought that their singing, testifying, or teaching a Sunday school class could please God. The national did not realize that it was the missionary's gasoline generator that gave power to the light bulb. Faith must be attached to God, just as the light must be attached to the generating plant.

God is the source of faith. But God is more than just a generating plant. He designed the system, built it, and keeps it running. When it comes to faith, God is everything. God even created the switch (faith) that we flip on to get light.

Some ridicule our faith, because they have flipped the switch, so to speak, and got no light. Because they read the Bible or did some other Christian acts and got no results, they say, "I knew it wouldn't work." And in that statement, they deny the faith they need to get light. When they are asked to try the switch, they protest, "I tried it once and it did not work," or "I had a friend who tried and didn't get it, so I know it won't work for me."

Light does not come from the switch; one must put faith in the whole system. Faith is somewhat like accepting the existence of electricity, the necessity of keeping the wires in place, and learning how to connect into the power plant. But most important, there are conditions to faith, just as there are conditions to getting light in the room. When all of the conditions are properly met and the switch is turned on, there will be light.

Then there are Christians who walked by faith in the past, but now they do not have fellowship with God. They used to turn on the switch and get light. They prayed and God answered their prayers. When they preached, souls came to the altar. When they taught Sunday school, little boys were converted and later became preachers. But something happened. Sin came into their lives or they allowed something to destroy their fellowship with God. Now when they go to the switch there is no light. The power lines have been cut and they do not have fellowship with God. Some pretend the light is on. Others make excuses, "God let me down." They may rationalize that they trusted God and he did not come through. These people want light, but have forgotten how to meet the condition explained in God's Word. Some try to bargain with God, "I've got to see the light first, then I'll turn on the switch."

There may exist a generating plant, wires, the light fixture in the ceiling, and the switch on the wall. But to have light, there must be an act—someone must turn on the switch. Faith is the link between the riches of God and our spiritual poverty. The spiritual lines are humming with power but we will remain defeated if we do not act in faith.

The act of faith begins with certain intellectual facts. We must know what God will do (Romans 10:17; Mark 1:15;

2 Timothy 2:25), then we must make a commitment based on what we know (John 1:37, 2 Thessalonians 2:13). This involves more than the mind. It involves also our wills. Specifically, this involves a decision. We decide to walk across the room and switch on the light.

Faith is living out the truths of the Bible. Many years ago as I visited an elderly woman in the hospital, she looked up and asked, "How can I get more faith?"

I was a young minister, just turned twenty years old, very unsure of my ecclesiastical position. I was embarrassed when someone asked a question that I could not answer. When the lady asked, "How can I get more faith?" she challenged my ministry.

Without closing my eyes, I prayed and asked God to give me an answer. Then God brought to mind a verse I had committed to memory, "Faith cometh by hearing, and hearing by the word of God" (Romans 10:17). I told her if she wanted to get more faith, she must get more of the Word of God in her heart. The secret to growing faith is in the Word of God.

But faith does not come just because we read Scripture. Faith is more than a rational understanding of God that comes from understanding the Scriptures, although that can be a first step. If we want more faith, we should read the Scripture, memorize verses, meditate on them, and allow the Word of God to influence every part of our being. But we must take the Bible a step further. Remember, the Scripture is more than an accurate book that communicates God's message to us. The Word of God is the written expression of the divine Word of God who is Jesus Christ. Jesus, the incarnate Word of God, is found in the Bible, the inspired Word of God. When we memorize Scripture, we allow God's Son to dwell in our hearts by faith (Ephesians 3:17) and to control our thoughts, desires, and, ultimately, to direct our actions.

Hence to have more faith, we must have Jesus Christ abiding in our hearts as he has commanded, ". . . abide in me, and my words abide in you" (John 15:7).

If we want valid faith, we must be convinced beyond all doubt that God is altogether worthy of our trust. The basis of our confidence is that the Spirit of God has convicted us of sin, we have experienced conversion, and now we have the peace of God that goes beyond understanding. This inner transformation is an experience that grounds our lives in confidence. As a result, we will have solid faith grounded in assurance. For saving faith we do not need support evidence, such as rationalism, pragmatic affirmation, or scientific research. Saving faith produces an inner knowledge that is *a priori*, that which needs no proof. It is the result of the Holy Spirit speaking directly to our hearts through the Word. This does not mean that our knowledge of the Word of God will not be rational or in some cases pragmatic. But our faith will not come through these means. Our faith will come from God.

Faith is not grounded in our emotions or desires. Our conversion is based on the Word of God, which is the revelation of God. Because the Bible speaks directly to us, we do not need emotional affirmation to prove its authority. As we read its words, the Spirit of God enlightens our blind eyes and causes us to comprehend the message of Scripture, "Comparing spiritual things with spiritual" (1 Corinthians 2:13). As the Word of God kindles an awareness within us, the validity of its testimony is affirmed.

In the light of the above, how foolish to try in our own effort to believe God. Faith is not our ability to persuade ourselves that up is not down, or that something will come to pass when we wish hard enough. The promises of God are as good as the One who made them.

Faith is not an incredible quality of a few noble Christians. Faith is attainable by all who trust God. Nor is faith limited to those with a Ph.D.'s knowledge of God. Sometimes the faith of a small child will be rewarded even more than that of a professor of theology. Remember,

Jesus said, "Except you have faith as a little child. . . ."

Faith cannot be measured by how much knowledge we have of God. Our faith is measured by the way we use our knowledge. If we put 100 percent of our knowledge to work with 100 percent of our ability, backed up with 100 percent of our trust, we can move the mountains that face us. As that faith grows, we can trust God to move larger and larger mountains.

There is a difference between natural faith and Bible faith, even though they are similar in expression. Natural faith is a child jumping into the arms of his parent because he trusts him. Natural faith is sitting on a chair because one trusts it to hold him, or switching on a light to illuminate a room. But Bible faith is more. When we put trust in God, it is because God gives us that faith. Such faith "is the gift of God" (Ephesians 2:8, 9).

THREE
SAVING FAITH

Faith is a gift bestowed upon us by the gracious God, the nature of which is to lay hold on Christ, whom God before did give for a ransom to redeem sinners. John Bunyan

Say-It-Faith begins with saving faith, which is simply looking to Jesus Christ for salvation. Salvation involves knowing the gospel, sincerely trusting God with all the feelings of the heart, and responding by an act of the will. Before a person can exercise Say-It-Faith, he must have saving faith as a foundation on which to build his Christianity. "But without faith it is impossible to please him; for he that cometh to God must believe that he is, and that he is a rewarder of them that diligently seek him" (Hebrews 11:6).

Dwight L. Moody, the famous evangelist, proclaimed that faith was the greatest power in the universe. He preached that simple belief in Jesus Christ could transform an individual, could dry up a drunk, or take the bitterness out of a failing marriage.

A man came to Moody and said, "What you preach is absurd. You preach that men have only to believe, and the whole course of their life will be changed." The man disagreed. He did not think that belief was that powerful or that important.

"I can change your mind in less than two minutes," stated Moody.

"No, you cannot," maintained the man.

Moody said, "Let us make sure that we understand each other. You say that belief will not change men's actions?"

"Yes," said the critic.

"Supposing," Moody said, "a man should put his head in that door and yell that the auditorium was on fire. What would you do?"

"I would get out immediately."

"Oh . . ." replied Moody, "when you believe the house is on fire you will take a new course of action."

Belief is the foundation of Christianity. For approximately 2,000 years the greatest miracles have occurred through faith. Lives have been changed, financial disasters have been averted, and families have been reunited. Of all the influences in the world, the greatest influence on the greatest number of people over the longest period of time is Christianity. And the power of Christianity is faith.

Saving faith is both simple and complex. Faith is as simple as a drowning man reaching for a rope, a child taking a step, or a sinner looking to Jesus Christ. Faith is simple belief. But on the other hand, saving faith is complex, setting in motion all the judicial machinery of heaven. The ultimate purpose of God is activated by faith. But eternal consequences are not gotten as easily as an impulsive purchase at the discount department store. To be saved a person must have proper knowledge, a proper emotion, and a proper decision of the will, so not everything that is called faith is proper faith.

Faith is both easy and difficult—easy, because it takes no energy to believe. As a matter of fact, faith is as easy as resting in a chair; one no longer holds himself up but lets the chair support his weight. And that is how some people get saved. They simply say, "I believe." On the other hand, others seem to work at getting saved. They pray with all sincerity and serve God with all intensity. They love God with all their hearts, and the intensity of their Christian life is usually a measure of the depth of their salvation.

A man came to Dwight L. Moody and said, "I can't believe." Moody knew the problem was with the man's attitude and not the content of Christianity.

Moody said, "Whom?"

"I don't know what you mean," the man said to Moody, "I said I cannot believe."

"You do not believe whom?" Moody asked again.

"You do not understand me, Mr. Moody, I said I cannot believe."

Each time Moody answered him, "Whom?" the man at first got angry, then began to squirm.

Out of desperation the man said, "I have a great many intellectual difficulties; there are a great many things I cannot believe."

Finally, Mr. Moody pointed out, "It is not God that you cannot believe, it is your ability to believe. Lack of faith is not God's problem; lack of faith is your internal problem. You do not have the ability to believe." When someone complains about his inability to believe, it is his neglect of seeking God and finding the road to everlasting life.

John stated clearly, "But these are written, . . . that believing ye might have life through his name" (John 20:31). God would not command a man to believe if man did not have the ability. But the verse shows two sides of this dilemma. First, natural faith is not enough to save a man. It takes supernatural help to enable a man to believe in God: "These are written, that ye might believe." Man needs help because the natural heart, which includes natural faith, rejects God and rebels against salvation. Supernatural faith, which is saving faith, is a gift from God (Ephesians 2:8, 9).

The second truth of the verse is seen in the source of faith, "These are written. . . ." Supernatural faith is given to man by the Word of God. So when a person says he cannot believe, we should tell him that he is correct. Then we should take him to the Scriptures, which is the instrument by which God implants faith in his heart (Romans 10:17).

Crying out to God is not sufficient for saving faith. Some people cry out to God because they are scared of dying or because they have problems in their lives. Fear is not a basis for faith, but fear can motivate a man to faith if the Word of God is in his heart. Faith, more than crying out to God, is turning one's whole life over to him on the basis of the Word of God.

FAITH BEGINS WITH ITS OBJECT

There seems to be a difference between "believe that" and "believe in." In the first place, a person may say, "I believe that it will rain," meaning he has a personal opinion. An opinion, like a hunch, is one's belief. But it usually is not based on a careful weighing of the evidence that leads to a commitment of the person's life, based on the information in question.

On the other hand, when a person says, "I believe in," he is speaking of a commitment to the information in focus. When a man believes in his friend, he has experienced oneness with another person and there is a basis of trustworthiness. The friendship is weighed and proven.

When a man "believes that" a thing is true, it involves his inner knowledge. When a man "believes in" a thing, it involves the credibility of the thing outside himself.

When a man "believes that" a thing is true, it involves only a mental acquaintance with truth. When a man "believes in" a thing, it involves his determination to act on what he knows.

When the Bible uses the word *trust* (Old Testament) or *believe* (New Testament), it is usually connected to the preposition *in,* such as "trust *in* the Lord" or "believe *in* Jesus Christ." Hence, the importance is not the person's ability to have faith, but the object of faith.

The Old Testament word for faith, *emunah,* usually refers to "believe in." It meant that a person had examined and experienced the truth so he had a basis for his belief. When the Old Testament had faith *(emunah)* in God, it meant that the person had examined and experienced God, and put his trust in him. God was real to him and he had heard the voice of God.

Emunah, which occurs 152 times in the Old Testament, demands total reliance upon the Lord as, "Trust in the Lord with all thine heart" (Proverbs 3:5). Other synonyms for *trust* that appear in the Hebrew parallelism are the words "trust in the Lord . . . delight thyself in the Lord . . . commit thy ways unto the Lord" (Psalm 37:3-5). *Emunah* is connected with our popular word *amen* and the word for truth, *emeth.* It means that in our hearts we say *amen* to the truth, hence we put our trust in it.

When a person is trusting the Lord he is taking refuge in God, as in the case of Ruth who left her homeland and became a citizen of Israel, the household of faith. Boaz noted her faith and said, "The Lord recompense thy work, and full reward be given thee of the Lord God of Israel, under whose wings thou art come to trust" (Ruth 2:12).

Faith is measured by its object, not subjective effort. Too many people think they can have faith if they search hard enough for it, or if they try hard enough to believe. Their faith is like the little girl who wanted it to stop raining so she could go outside and play. Her mother told her, "If you wish hard enough it will stop raining." No matter how hard the little girl strained, it did not stop raining. She tried hard, like some people try to believe, but self-effort will not get results.

For faith to save, it must have the correct object, which is Jesus Christ. Paul told the Philippian jailer, "Believe on the Lord Jesus Christ, and thou shalt be saved" (Acts 16:31).

First, saving faith has as its object the Father. "Have faith in God" (Mark 11:22). But also included in saving faith is belief in Jesus Christ. Jesus reminded his disciples, "Believe in God, believe also in me" (John 14:1).

The Holy Spirit is the agent of faith. An agent is the one who acts on the behalf of another and the Holy Spirit acts on behalf of Jesus Christ to plant faith in a person's heart. The Holy Spirit is the one who initiates the faith process by convicting or causing a sinner to see his sin (John 16:8, 9). By the work of conviction, the Holy Spirit is working in a sinner's heart to draw him to the Savior. The work of conviction is not just to make a sinner sorry for his sin, although it does involve emotions (2 Corinthians 7:10). The Holy Spirit is the agent who works in the sinner's heart to make him aware that he is a sinner, that Jesus is God's standard of righteousness, and that the cross paid the debt for sin (John 16:8).

As an agent, the Holy Spirit will not speak of himself, but he will magnify his client, Jesus Christ. He will point all men to the Savior (John 16:13). As such, the Holy Spirit begins the work of faith in the human heart, causing the Word of God to grow and bring forth faith.

When the sinner responds, the Holy Spirit gives him the gift of faith (Ephesians 2:8, 9); therefore, no man recognizes Jesus as the Christ without the Holy Spirit (1 John 4:2). Finally, if a person does not have the Holy Spirit, he is not a Christian (Romans 8:9).

The Bible is the instrument of faith. When Paul said, "Faith cometh by hearing, and hearing by the word of God" (Romans 10:17), he was saying that the Bible is the tool in the hand of God to bring forth faith in the human heart.

Just as a carpenter uses a hammer to build things, so God uses the Bible as an instrument to build faith in the human heart. When a preacher quotes the Bible, God uses it to break rocks of unbelief or to cut out prejudice and ignorance (Acts 5:33).

Jesus taught, "The seed is the word of God" (Mark 8:11). The Bible is called *seed* because it has life inherent in it. A seed may appear dead, but there is embryonic life within. The seed is sown in the cold, dark earth. There it begins to rot and disintegrate. To germinate, the outer shell of the seed must die in the soil. The soil itself does not have the power to bring forth the grain and fruit. Fruit comes from the seed. Whenever the farmer wants to reap wheat, he must sow wheat. It does not make any difference how rich his soil. Only what he puts in the ground will come up.

So, when the Word of God is planted in our hearts, it brings forth faith. Very simply, the seed which is the Word of God builds our faith.

However, there are several different kinds of soil. Some soil is rich, black, and life-producing. Other ground is sandy and arid. The rich soil could be likened to a searching mind while the arid land is similar to a skeptical heart. What makes the plant grow is water and fertilizer on the seed, and the supply of life from the sunshine.

Just as a seed takes time to germinate in the soil, so the Word of God must have time to work in the human heart. This time of germination is called *conviction*—the sinner is convinced that the message is true. After a period of time, the seed bursts forth out of the ground into the sunlight. Just so, the seed of the Word of God breaks forth into conversion. The Bible is the instrument that produces faith in the sinner, who is born again by "the word of truth" (James 1:18). Peter describes the process, "Being born again, not of corruptible seed, but of incorruptible, by the word of God" (1 Peter 1:23). In another place, Peter said that this conversion produces a new nature which comes by the instrumentality of Scripture, "Whereby are given unto us exceeding great and precious promises: that by these ye might be partakers of the divine nature" (2 Peter 1:4). Therefore, the Holy Spirit, the *agent of faith,* uses the Bible, the *instrument of faith,* to produce saving faith in the heart. Saving faith produces a new nature in the new convert (2 Corinthians 5:17) and he is given eternal life (John 5:24).

In the parable of the sower there were weeds that killed faith. The weeds are worldliness that will choke out belief in God. Also, birds came and plucked the seed away from the soil, as Satan comes to pluck away and destroy our faith. And in another application, Jesus described seed that fell upon the pathway. It would not grow, in the same way that a hard heart that is callous to God will not grow faith.

If we want our faith to grow, we must have a tender heart towards God. This involves digging out the weeds of worldliness, resisting the devil who steals the Word of God, and breaking up the fallow soil by repentance. This illustration reveals that faith is not a thing that is present in our hearts before we receive the Word of God. Faith comes from the Word of God and must grow in our hearts. It takes both the Word of God and the willing heart to build a life of faith.

THREE STEPS TO FAITH
Good works are more natural for us than faith. When we try to work our way to heaven, we do not give our whole lives to God. By good works, we give God only what we do not want. We think we can perform good works, yet keep secret sin in our hearts. We think we can give money, yet hold on to spots of rebellion toward God. But, when we put faith in Jesus Christ, we trust our entire lives to him. And since the sum total of man's person is intellect, emotion, and will, then faith is the outgrowth of

what we *know,* what we *feel,* and what we *do.* Faith is a response of the sum total of our lives to God. The three human steps of faith are: (1) knowing, (2) feeling, and (3) doing. But, we must read carefully, for intellectual faith can never save; feelings are no foundation for belief; and doing only leads to legalism. Yet when these three steps are interfaced with the Word of God, faith is the result.

Knowledge of God and his plan is the foundation of faith. Intellectual faith has never saved anyone, but intellectual knowledge is one of the foundations for saving faith. Intellectual faith is measured by what a man knows about the historical facts of Christianity. It is not a matter of the emotions or the will, but simply knowledge about God.

All men everywhere are commanded to know God, but intellectual assent to a truth is not the same as personal trust in that truth. The character of God is our foundation for faith. Therefore, the more we know about God's character, the more faith we can have. When we know him as God, the mighty Creator of the world, we realize he is the source of all things. Also, when we know God as Jehovah, the self-existing being, we know he exists in himself and for himself. When we know that God sent his Son, the Lord Jesus Christ, as the Savior to die for the sins of the world, we know the source of salvation is in him. When we realize God is Creator, the self-existing One and the Savior, then we have a basis of our faith in God.

It is only natural that we will put our faith in trustworthy people and distrust those with poor character. Hence, when we know the nature and works of God, we will put our trust in him.

Because God dwells in eternal mystery, no one ever comes to fully understand God. Nor will we ever have perfect faith all the time. But, even though God has not revealed everything about himself, there are certain things we can know about him. God will always do what he has promised to do. When we accept his testimony, we are exercising intellectual faith. This rational understanding will not save, but it will become the basis of salvation.

One can believe a thing is true only when he possesses adequate evidence to back up his knowledge. Then he has a foundation on which to build faith. If someone raises a question whether the Word of God is true and accurate, the Bible becomes its own proof. As we read the Bible, we realize it is a consistent book. No part of the Scriptures denies or contradicts another part. In that way, the Word of God is like a circle; it is consistent in every part—a perfect book. But, we also find the Word of God corresponds to life. The description of life in the Bible corresponds to the way life really is. The Word of God tells us of the influence of sin in the world, and we know it is true because of our experience. Also, the Word of God tells how to get happiness and we know it is true because we have entered into abundant life. Because the events of daily life give evidence to the truth of the Bible, we know it is the Word of God. The Bible, which is the source of objective faith, strengthens our intellectual faith. Again, this is a *rational* understanding, but not the same as *saving* faith.

God's Word is true, whether or not we believe it. Also, the promise of God remains the same, whether or not we act on it. And our faith is useless until we attach it to the Word of God, because God responds only to those who know and recognize him, and the only way to know God is through his Word.

The Bible speaks of personal faith as being more than a knowledge of the Word of God. When one comes into a theoretical possession of the knowledge of God, he may believe the existence of God involuntarily. But, this knowledge does not save him. For example, a person may be told that his nation is losing the war. He accepts the facts involuntarily and has no ability to stop believing what he has heard. But his knowledge is not personal unless he becomes involved, works in a factory, purchases a war bond, or volunteers for action. Then his knowledge goes beyond academic information.

In the same way, a man can be told that he is a sinner (Romans 3:23), and that as a sinner, he will be punished in hell (Romans 6:23). He accepts these facts involuntarily because he knows his experience and has no reason to refrain from believing what he has heard. But, saving faith goes beyond knowledge. Saving faith involves making a commitment to do something based on knowledge. Then, the person moves from intellectual awareness towards salvation.

Effective faith deals with the will or the volition of man. Paul described this, "Ye have obeyed from the heart" (Romans 6:17). When a man believes that he is going to hell, and cries out for mercy and claims the blood of Jesus Christ to save him, he has obeyed the commands of the Word of God. He has obeyed from the heart. This is experiential faith. He is willing to act on what he knows.

Intellectual faith is the basis for volitional faith. In the first step, the person believes in the existence of God, that the Bible is God's Word, that Jesus has shed his blood on the cross for the sins of mankind, and that God will save those who call upon him. Knowledge of the plan of salvation will not save a man. By faith he must respond to the above statements of truth.

Faith is effective by its object, as the woman who sneaked into the crowd to touch Jesus Christ. "For she said, 'If I may touch but his clothes, I shall be whole'" (Mark 5:28). She recognized that Jesus was the answer to her problem. She needed healing, and she knew that Jesus could heal her. She placed her faith in Jesus Christ, but expressed it wrongly. She thought the answer was touching the Master.

But after she was healed, Jesus said it was not the touch that had healed her. "Thy faith hath made thee whole"

(Mark 5:34). He reaffirmed the source of her faith—she came to Jesus Christ. He corrected the intellectual assessment of her faith—it was not her touch. Today, many people think that Jesus is magical. They want to touch him with their hands, as they would a relic. They think that by some physical means, by going to church, or by singing in the choir they make contact with him. Other people think they can get faith by visiting the family cemetery or doing something religious. Their problem is that they want to do something in the physical realm, as the woman wanted to touch him. But Jesus told the woman, "Thy faith hath made thee whole."

Our faith is measured by its object, God, and not our inner desires. Therefore, when our knowledge of God is wrong, it must be corrected. So, to have faith in God, we must know him accurately; and we must act on what we know about him.

But our knowledge of God does not mean we will know all things, for no one can ever know everything about God. He is infinite and we are limited in our understanding. We cannot know all there is to know about God, but first we must know the essentials of salvation, and, second, we must act with all of our hearts on what we know.

Emotions are the reflections of faith. Faith also involves the emotions, as either a cause or effect, in the process of conversion. As quickly as we mention the emotional aspect of faith, we must add that faith is not an emotional feeling, nor does the intensity of our emotions make our faith efficacious. Yet we cannot remove emotions from the trust process. Jesus laid down the condition that a person must, "love the Lord thy God with all thy heart, and with all thy soul, and with all thy mind. This is the first and great commandment. And the second is like unto it, Thou shalt love thy neighbour as thyself" (Matthew 22:37-39). In this command Jesus did not suggest partial love. As the young girl at the marriage altar wants all of the love of her future husband, so Jesus Christ wants complete love from those who are joined to him in salvation. Sometimes our emotions drive us to the Word of God. In this sense, emotions bring us to conversion. Other times our emotions are stirred by the Word of God. In this sense, emotions are the result of conversion.

One of the opposites of faith is fear, which is also an emotion. Just as we express faith by the emotion of love, so we quench faith when we are fearful. The disciples were out on the lake when the storm came up. These were not weekend fishermen but veteran journeymen. They had seen many storms on the Sea of Galilee. When they cried out in fear, Jesus rebuked them, "Why has fear filled your heart?" Fear was only the natural reaction to the intensity of the storm. They had walked with the Son of God and seen him perform mighty miracles, yet they could not trust him at that moment.

Lest anyone think that fear is not an emotion, let him feel his mouth go dry and let him experience the inability of the mind to function properly when he sees a snake or loses control of his car on wet pavement. In that moment he has experienced an emotion that controlled his entire reaction to life. He experienced fear. It is difficult to trust God when fear controls our perspective of life.

No one fully understands the depths of his emotions, nor can anyone fully control them. Even the man who appears to have ice water in his veins and eyes of steel cannot always control his heart. If no one can completely control emotions, nor understand emotions, how is faith related to emotions? Since a person cannot experience all emotions, those feelings that he does experience must be brought to the foot of the cross. Also, since a person cannot know all of his true emotions, what he experiences about himself must be given to God in total trust.

Sometimes emotions are the result of faith. Paul said, "For in Jesus Christ neither circumcision availeth any thing, neither uncircumcision; but faith which worketh by love" (Galatians 5:6). Here faith becomes in the human personality a new law that produces love. Jesus said we must love God with all our hearts with love that comes as a result of faith. When a person invites Jesus Christ into his life (John 1:12), he receives the source of love that enables him to love God with all his heart. The sinner is filled with divine power to love, with which he can meet the divine expectations.

There are problems in trying to relate feelings and faith. A person can feel exhilarated one day and depressed the next day with very little explanation for the difference. Such a person can be controlled by his emotions, rather than controlling his feelings. Sometimes people are depressed because they desire to be depressed. They have allowed their wills to control their emotions. On other occasions, emotions are controlled by a person's intellectual understanding. For instance, we love some people because we admire them. God does not save just the emotionally healthy person. He saves anyone who casts himself upon his mercy.

But emotions are tied to faith, as good works are the natural outgrowth of faith. Just as a person's faith without works is dead, so a person's faith without the accompaniment of emotions is barren.

The Philippian jailer rejoiced in his belief (Acts 16:34), giving illustration of what Paul later described as joy and peace in believing (Romans 15:13). At another place, Paul tied the emotions of joy to the noun *faith,* "joy of faith" (Philippians 1:25).

The outward expression of emotions is not always equal to an inner reality. Some people experience feelings of love for God, but the feelings do not show outwardly. Others may laugh, shout, or express love in an obvious emotional display. The same is true for the emotions of guilt, joy, conviction, or worship. The rule to help guide us is that a person will usually come to Jesus Christ at the level of his own emotional response. We should not be surprised if a person with a mathematical approach to life does not respond with an outward display of feeling. Whether he shows outward emotions is unimportant; the fact that he responds to God is all that matters.

Once a woman told me she was trying, but could not be saved. The more I talked to her, the more I realized she was seeking an emotional feeling. She mistakenly thought she had to have unbounded joy, unending happiness, and a thrill at conversion, similar to the excitement she would feel at a circus.

I quoted several verses to her. She said to me, "I trust the Lord Jesus Christ with all my heart, but I don't feel any different."

I said to her, "Do not seek feelings. Seek the Savior. There is no command in the Word of God that says you must have a feeling, even though some people get a feeling after they are saved."

After quoting several verses to her, I put my hand out and said, "I ask you to express a simple act of your will. I want you to reach out and shake my hand as a sign that you are trusting Jesus Christ as your Savior. Just as you believe I am offering my hand to you, I want you to believe Jesus is offering salvation to you."

I held out my hand, but she did not take it.

Finally I said, "I want you to receive Jesus and let your feelings take care of themselves." I kept my hand extended. She waited for a few moments, then reached out and took it.

She prayed with hesitation, the words were unsure, as though she was searching for the correct words. When she finished she said, "I did it." As we continued speaking, she repeatedly said, "I did it." Her conversion was not one of intellectual knowledge, as she had known the plan of salvation, but could not believe. Her conversion was not one of emotions, for she had sought an experience, but could not gain it, although I sensed the emotion of confidence after her prayer. Her conversion was characterized by a decision of the will. When she was faced with the decision of actually reaching out and taking my hand, she acted rationally and placed her trust in Jesus Christ. Six months after her conversion, I saw this woman again, and she again repeated to me, "I did it."

The will must act in faith. The third aspect of the experience of faith deals with our will or volition. What place does willpower have in developing faith?

Some people mistakenly think that if they have a strong will, they can develop faith. They are reasoning that if they have willpower to resist fattening food or the willpower to jog ten miles a day, they can have strong faith. A strong will is another way of saying "self-control." Whereas self-control is necessary for faith, the person who has a weak will can develop faith, and sometimes develop more productive faith. The success of faith is not measured by our personality but by the object of our faith, which is God.

Faith comes to those who cease self-effort. When we are going to sit on a chair, we must cease depending on our muscles to hold us up. We must rest completely on the chair. After we know the chair will hold us, we must, by an act of our will, decide to sit down. Our will has been the controlling element of our life, but now we turn the control of our bodies over to the chair. So faith turns the control of our lives over to Jesus Christ. Paul noted, "Whereas ye obey from the heart" (Romans 6:17), describing salvation as an act of the will whereby a person is obedient to the gospel.

The will is involved in repentance. When a person turns "to God from idols" (1 Thessalonians 1:10) he has made a choice against his old life and has made a choice for a new life with God.

The Greek word for "repentance," *metanoya,* first means "to know with oneself." When a person repents, he comes to a correct knowledge of himself. He knows what he has been doing is wrong, so repentance involves a knowledgeable act. Self-knowledge also knows the acts are wrong. The second aspect of repentance, *metanoya,* means "to change the mind." What one knows in the mind becomes the basis for a volitional act—a person chooses Jesus Christ.

On the surface, an expression of the will seems like a simple operation. Someone says, "Would you like to go to town?" and a person answers, "No." This is simply an act of the will to reject an invitation. On the other hand, someone asks, "Would you like a glass of milk?" and the person answers, "Yes." Even though it seems like a simple act, the exercise of the will involves the emotions. We choose milk because we like it or we choose not to go downtown because we are discouraged.

The exercise of the will is also tied to bodily function. We are tired, therefore, we do not go downtown.

Sometimes, the exercise of the will is tied to the intellect. We know that someone is coming to see us, so we choose not to go downtown.

Finally, the exercise of the will goes beyond all of these. Sometimes it is based on subconscious motivations. We may not know why we choose milk over water, but we do.

No one fully understands the will and how it operates. Also, no one can fully control his will. The man who has said "No!" a thousand times, on the spur of the moment says "Yes!" The man who has been making good choices, suddenly makes an erratic one. Human nature being what it is, the exercising of the will is difficult to understand. So, where does that leave faith?

In the act of faith, we must completely yield our wills to God. However, in that act, we may not understand all that we are doing. No one can completely yield himself because no one has full control of himself. We still have a sinful nature. But when it comes to faith, we cannot yield what we are not aware of in our nature, but all that we do know at the moment must be yielded to him.

In the act of faith, we may not control tomorrow, but we can yield today to Christ. In the act of faith, we may not be able to control our emotional discouragement next week, but we can yield our mood today. In the act of faith, we may not intellectually know what will happen next year, but we can trust him today.

Faith and repentance walk hand in hand. Faith is not repentance, and repentance is not faith, but we cannot have one without the other.

Faith involves the surrender of the soul to God. It is impossible to have faith when we continually give ourselves to sin. When we read in Scripture, "Repent ye, and believe the gospel" (Mark 1:15), we see how faith and repentance work together. Faith is the appropriation of God while repentance is getting our hearts ready for his occupation.

It is absurd to think that Christ can come and dwell in our hearts without a commensurate act of repentance whereby we volitionally repent of sin. Without biblical repentance, there is no saving faith. Repentance is not an actual victory over sin. If that were so, repentance would be our own effort and a result of our good works. But repentance is bringing every sin to the feet of the Lord Jesus Christ so that he can give victory. And how do we do that? By faith. First of all, we realize he is faithful to forgive sin and to cleanse from all unrighteousness. Second, we trust Jesus to make us free from sin. And, third, the more eager we are to become free from sin, the more we are brought near to God who gives us deliverance over sin.

Therefore, in salvation, we began by repentance and we end by repentance, for we must completely turn from sin and turn to God. But also, we begin by faith and end by faith. First, we begin by faith which cultivates a consciousness of God. Faith puts our eyes on Jesus Christ. We end by faith, recognizing that God must not only save us, but that he also sanctifies us.

In essence, repentance and faith become one action,

even though we view it from two perspectives. Just as a man must leave one room as he walks through a door into a second room, faith is an ongoing action of the soul in turning from sin to Jesus Christ.

CONCLUSION
Theoretical knowledge about God is the basis for salvation, but no one has ever been saved on knowledge alone. Repentance may lead to faith, but no one has ever been saved on repentance alone. Knowledge of God and repentance from sin are conditions for faith, but are not faith themselves. And faith is the condition for salvation, but faith itself is not salvation. Saving faith is the volitional response of the person who turns to Christ from sin with all of his emotional being. He turns to Christ according to the biblical plan of salvation, so that Jesus Christ comes into his life, giving him all the benefits of regeneration.

FOUR
LIVING BY FAITH

Faith is not a human notion or a dream as some take it to be; faith is a divine work in us. Oh, it is a living, creative, active, mighty thing, this faith. Martin Luther

Say-It-Faith that moves mountains does not come overnight. A person might develop his ability to trust God by applying the principles of Scripture to daily life. Living by faith involves trusting God for more than money. It involves trusting God for joy, victory, and wisdom to do his will. "For we walk by faith, not by sight" (2 Corinthians 5:7). Those who have practiced living by faith are those who can move obstacles as big as mountains by faith.

After my conversion, I turned down a scholarship funded by the Junior Chamber of Commerce that would have paid my tuition and fees to Armstrong Junior College in Savannah, Georgia. Yet, at the time of my salvation I knew God was calling me into full-time Christian service—immediately and suddenly. I rejected the scholarship and prepared to attend Columbia (S.C.) Bible College, with very little money in the bank. My parents were not able to help me financially. We lived in a small rented house for which they paid twenty-five dollars a month. My father, who later died an alcoholic, did not get a large salary. My mother worked in a school cafeteria to help pay for my education, so going to college was a step of faith for me.

At Columbia Bible College I encountered people who introduced me to the life of faith. There I learned that God commanded, "For we walk by faith, not by sight" (2 Corinthians 5:7). Money is important to a boy growing up with few material things. To the people at Columbia Bible College, the life of faith meant trusting God to supply money and all the other needs of life. It was not that they did not work hard, or that they did not have luxuries. They just had a different priority concerning money. They looked beyond money to God, the source and satisfaction of life. They depended upon God for everything, including spiritual victory over sin. I frankly struggled with the life of faith, often more defeated than victorious.

Columbia Bible College had always been a strong missionary institution, and most of the students went abroad sponsored by "faith mission boards." At Columbia, a number of sermons challenged me to live by faith, most of which made me feel very inadequate. I wanted to be a man of great faith, such as George Muller and David Brainerd. I wanted to move mountains through faith. Yet I was a seventeen-year-old freshman with no resources but Almighty God who had called me into the ministry. So I began to pray for money—long, often, sincerely. Some answers came in unusual ways.

Mrs. O. M. Alcorn, of the Bonnabella Presbyterian Chapel in Savannah, told her class of children how I had stepped out by faith and given up a scholarship in order to serve Christ. They determined to help me. Those juniors caught crabs in the salt creeks around Bonnabella, cooked them in a tub over an open flame in a backyard, then sold them for a nickel apiece, door to door. When I received their first envelope with fifteen dollars for my room and board, I was overwhelmed. I felt unworthy to receive that money and wanted to mail it right back. But those young people loved me and wanted to help me train for the Lord's work.

I had wished that God would provide for my needs through some millionaire who could give the money and not miss it. I knew the children's gift came from God, but it did not come the way I would have chosen.

As I began to live by faith, I learned that humility is tied to faith. During that year, several small gifts came from various sources, but no great answer to prayer, no large gift from an anonymous donor. I wanted to move mountains and hear the crash of splintering rock or splintering timbers, but here I was with a shovel, moving one small pile of dirt at a time! One aunt sent five dollars, another sent ten dollars, and so the process continued through the year. My mother sent some money, but I did not want her to have to work to help me. But God does not always answer our prayers the way we desire. I left college at the end of the first year with all my bills paid. I am forever grateful for Columbia Bible College providing an atmosphere where I would experience the life of faith.

When I went back for my second year of college, I again faced the crisis of how to pay my bills. Under pressure, I struggled in prayer, begging God to meet my financial needs. At the beginning of that year, some outstanding Christian men of the Independent Presbyterian Church in Savannah, Georgia, informed me they would pay my room, board, and fees. At last I heard the rumble of rocks as God moved mountains. This took a tremendous amount of pressure off of me. I worked in the school dining room for twenty cents an hour to make pocket money. While I was living by faith, I knew it was not a triumphant faith. I knew God was answering my prayers. Each time I received a check or a gift, I knew it came from his hand. I was learning to live by faith, but through great struggle. Those years prepared me for what lay ahead.

Perhaps the greatest test of my faith came when in 1961

to 1965 I was president of Winnipeg Bible College, Canada. Taking this position involved courage to move to the frigid prairies of Manitoba. The cold winter in Canada set records—forty days in a row when the temperature did not get above 30° below zero. To obey Christ and go into that environment took faith.

Winnipeg Bible College was a "faith institution," and the financial policy stated in the college catalog was: "Full information without solicitation," which meant that the college prayed for finances, but did not ask individuals for money. There were forty-three students, with a budget of $23,000 the year before I became president. During my first year, the student body increased by 50 percent, which means we had sixty-one students. The debt was oppressive and the bills were staggering.

I had never run a business that large and had never raised the amounts of money needed there. Previously, when needed money did not come in, I simply sacrificed. That also meant that my family went without some luxuries or necessities of life. But Canada was different. Responsible for a faculty of five professors and three staff members who looked to me for their pay checks, I agonized when I had to call them in and say there was no money. But what else could I do? I recognized my lack of faith, and pleaded, cried, and inwardly bled.

On some occasions I prayed all night. I remember my family going to bed about sundown (on the Canadian prairie around 9:00 p.m. in the summer). I prayed all night until the sun came up in the morning. I felt I had victory, but had to learn that feeling victorious is entirely different from being victorious. After praying all night, I went to the mailbox, expecting to see stacks of letters, each stuffed with money. I do not recall the exact number, but I do recollect only two or three letters contained even small amounts of money.

I rationalized, "God answered my prayers, but it will take two or three days for the mail to reach the college."

But the same thing happened the next two days at the mailbox; only a couple of letters had small checks in them. God had led such giants as Hudson Taylor and George Muller to raise money by prayer and faith. I came to the conclusion that I did not have the gift of faith.

After such struggles with finances for two years, I announced to the board of directors that we should change our policy. Our former statement of "full information without solicitation" had worked for others but not for us. I felt we needed to use our gifts of leadership and administration. I told the board that I wanted to aggressively raise money, especially to pay off the $25,000 indebtedness of the college. I had strong vision, though my faith was weak.

I laid out a plan to raise money for past debts and future expenses. As I outlined a plan of fund-raising, the board backed my strategy. I began to interview individuals, asking them to give to the school. The first person was Sidney Smith, a wealthy grain broker in Winnipeg, known for his outstanding Christian philanthropy. After we had lunch, I presented Mr. Smith with the needs of Winnipeg Bible College. He took out his checkbook and wrote a check for $1,000. That gift turned around my attitude about raising money.

For the fortieth anniversary of the college, we organized the alumni, faculty, board, and students into an aggressive stewardship program. I divided people into teams, who approached those who had previously given to the college. Because of this successful program, we raised $50,000 and received a matching grant of $50,000 from the M-P Foundation of Toronto, Canada. In early years, I would have considered it lack of faith to ask for money. But I had grown in my understanding, and now consider solicitation an act of faith. It took faith to set a goal, enlist workers, print brochures, and carry out a program that involved over one hundred people who committed themselves to its success.

THE LAW OF FAITH

Some think Jerry Falwell is not living by faith because he asks for money. I probably thought that at one time, but today I realize it takes faith to set a financial goal, organize a financial campaign, and ask people for money. The way Dr. Falwell raises money reflects principles of faith. This does not mean that he is perfect or that everyone agrees with everything he does. But there are certain laws that are necessary in raising money if we would have the blessing of God in our endeavors.

Living by faith involves more than just getting money from God. Living by faith involves our total lives—time, talents, and treasure—every part of our lives must be controlled by God's laws if we live by faith. Getting money by faith is used to illustrate the life of faith because we usually understand it. Living by faith is overcoming discouragement, or raising our children properly. To live by faith, we must follow the laws of God's Word.

Some think the life of faith is following one's feelings, or waiting for the "inner voice of God" to speak. But the life of faith is more than this. If we want to live successfully by faith, we must know "the law of faith" (Romans 3:17).

To put the words *faith* and *law* together in one phrase seems contradictory. Throughout the Bible we are told that faith is free, while the law involves works. But the two words are not contradictory. "Law" simply means "principles or rules." When we read "the law of faith," it means there are principles by which we exercise faith. When we live by the law of faith, we live by God's plan. The law, in this sense, is an extension of the nature of God.

When the Bible says "the law is holy" (Romans 7:12), it means the law is an extension of God who is holy, just, and good. Paul also said "the law is spiritual" (Romans 7:12), which means the law is good. But no man has ever kept the law. Even Paul says, "I am carnal, sold unto sin" (Romans 7:14). When he tried to keep the law he cried out "I see another law in my members, warring against the law of my mind, and bringing me into captivity to the law of sin" (Romans 7:23). That law condemned him to death. And, according to James, if we break one law, we have broken them all (James 2:10). Once we break the law, we fall under its condemnation and influence. In contrast to the law of faith is the law of sin. Paul said, "I find then a law, that when I would do good, evil is present with me" (Romans 7:21).

But the law of faith overcomes the law of sin. This means we must follow the principles of faith to overcome evil. It is possible for one law to be more powerful than another. When a helium balloon floats, the law of aerodynamics indicates a "lighter than air object will float." Hence, the one law overcomes another law.

The law of faith pulls us toward God while the law of sin pulls us toward hell. The more powerful law supersedes the lesser law. Paul described this, "For the law of the Spirit of life in Christ Jesus hath made me free from the law of sin and death" (Romans 8:2). The Old Testament law is the lesser law, and when we live under it, we must be judged by it. But when we are saved, we no longer live by the law of the Old Testament. We live by the law of Christ (Galatians 6:2). Jesus Christ completely kept the law and fulfilled it (Matthew 5:17), then put it away in his death (Ephesians 2:15; Colossians 2:14).

Now Christ lives in us, as Paul wrote "that the righteousness of the law might be fulfilled in us, who walk not after the flesh but after the Spirit" (Romans 8:4). When we live by the law of faith, we know that we are not perfect. We know that we cannot keep the law, but we have direction in our walk of faith. The law of faith was never intended to make us good or condemn us, but to give us principles by which we express our faith.

PRINCIPLES OF FAITH

The Obvious Obedience Law. There are many good definitions of faith. Perhaps the most implicit is, "Faith is obedience to the Word of God." Although Jesus saw that his disciples had fished all night, he commanded, "Cast the net on the right side of the ship, and ye shall find" (John 21:6). In obedience to the command of Christ, the disciples fished on the other side and caught 153 fish, plus some more they could not even get into the boat. Their obedience to the command of Christ produced success. Remember, Jesus Christ is God, and all he spoke was the Word of God. Therefore, when the disciples obeyed his word, they exercised faith.

In the synagogue Jesus encountered a man with a withered hand. Everyone watched to see what Jesus would do. He commanded the man, "Stand forth" (Mark 3:3). Everyone was astounded at what he did, except the Pharisees, who were angry. Then the Bible says, "He had looked round about on them with anger, being grieved for the hardness of their hearts" (Mark 3:5). They did not have faith in Jesus, but the crippled man did. Then Jesus commanded, "Stretch forth thine hand" (3:5). In obedience to Jesus' command, the Word of God, the man stretched forth his hand and it was restored as the other. His act of faith brought healing.

The Divine Assistance Law. If we want results from our faith, we must act in harmony with the Lord. The act of faith is also spoken of in the Scripture as the work of the Holy Spirit. "We have the same spirit of faith" (2 Corinthians 4:13). Most commentaries interpret the word *spirit* to mean the Holy Spirit. Thus, when we act on our faith, we are acting with the Holy Spirit who works in our hearts.

The working of the Holy Spirit always leads to more faith toward God. Also, faith is one of the fruits of the Holy Spirit (Galatians 5:22). In essence, when the Holy

Spirit works in our hearts, we are better able to trust in the Lord, which is faith.

Jesus said of the Holy Spirit, "Ye know him, for he dwelleth with you, and shall be in you" (John 14:17). Thus, the Holy Spirit was *with* people in the Old Testament, but in the New Testament the Holy Spirit dwells *in* the heart of every believer. Therefore, if we want more faith, we must let the Holy Spirit have more of our lives. Paul also describes this, "Be not drunk with wine . . . but be filled with the Spirit" (Ephesians 5:18).

The Sincerity Law. How does sincerity relate to faith? Some people say we must be extremely "sincere" if our faith is going to move God. This is a delusion. The Bible does not teach us that our faith becomes valid when we are sincere. False prophets are sincere in their preaching and teaching. Those who belong to a false religion pray with all the sincerity possible. Our faith is not measured by our sincerity, but by its object—Jesus Christ. But after we find the object of faith, we must "trust in the Lord with all thine heart" (Proverbs 3:5). Sincerity does not make our faith valid, but it does make it more effective in our relationship to God.

Dwight L. Moody told the story of the person who said, "I am sincere," adding, "but I do not have faith." Moody told him that he was an insult to God. "Suppose I said to you, I sincerely trust you, but do not believe a word you say." In essence, Moody was calling him a liar. He continued, "I wouldn't give much for sincerity if you do not believe a person's word."

Those who do not believe the Word of God are not sincerely searching for God. Jesus said, "If any man will do his will, he shall know of the doctrine" (John 7:17, see KJV). God wants us to trust him as little children. A little child will never say, "I love you, Mother, but I do not believe what you say."

The Word of God attaches great value to sincerity. It

teaches that we should love God and trust him with all of our hearts. Sincerity is that attitude of the heart by which we present ourselves to the Lord of the Bible, just as we are, neither better nor worse than we are. In contrast, insincere people make themselves either better than they are, or worse than they are.

To have faith, we must search for the Lord with all our hearts. But we say we have doubts. We ask, "How can I be sincere and still doubt?" To solve our problem, we do not have to search harder for faith; for the more we seek faith, usually the less we have it. In contrast, the more we search for the Lord, the more faith we will get. In our search, we will encounter our unbelief. What should we do when we face doubts? Should we mourn over our unbelief and give up? No. Should we act like "the power of positive thinkers," and try to puff up our faith, as one blows up a deflated tire? No! Should we wait until we have the right feelings? No! All these endeavors will not give us faith, no matter how sincere we are.

We must come to the Lord of the Bible with childlike sincerity. We must come with the attitude, "Lord, I believe in you—but I also recognize there is unbelief in my heart." If we can come this way, we are sincere, for we sincerely recognize our doubt.

What should we do with insincerity? When we have trouble with doubt in our hearts, we should confess it to the Lord. Sometimes I confess, "Lord, I love your Bible, but I am too selfish to read it." By the same confession a woman says, "Lord, I need daily communion with you, but I am too busy to pray." When we become truthful before God, we have taken a step towards maturity. The only place where we can overcome insincerity is in Jesus' presence. The only way we can overcome insecurity is by an honest confession of our hearts before God. And as we strive each day, we will obtain victory over insincerity. Then we can say with John, "This is the victory that overcometh the world, even our faith" (1 John 5:4).

The "Seed Faith" Law. Children learn to run long before their legs can carry them. They see their friends run and they decide to mimic them. Even the little baby toddles across the kitchen floor because of an inner desire to walk. And so we have a great desire to believe in God, long before we can move mountains. That is why God gives us commands for which we have no previous power. Yet when we submit to God, then the strength of God works through us. When Jesus said, "If ye have faith as a grain of mustard seed" (Matthew 17:20), he was describing the "seed faith" law. To paraphrase the Master's promise, "If your faith is infinitesimally small, but you trust God with the faith you have, then nothing is impossible to you because you can move mountains." We should not be discouraged with our little faith, but we should begin with the faith we have. If we cannot trust God for a churchwide revival, then we should trust him for one soul to be saved. If we cannot trust God for answered prayer, then we should trust him that he hears and forgives our sins.

The "One-Page-a-Day" Law. This book is the thirty-second one I have written. People who want to write usually ask me how I can write so much. I usually tell them, "If you can write a letter a day, you can write a sizeable book every year." The secret to writing is "one-page-a-day." I write my books by faith. I get a topic from my study or I see a spiritual need. By faith, I feel God would have me speak to that need. By faith, I do my research and write the biblical principles that will work in the church. By faith, I apply the journalistic lessons acquired from experience. But all of God's leading will not produce a book unless I discipline myself to write. By faith, I set an objective to write "one-page-a-day."

To accomplish our goals in life, we will need to discipline ourselves. Self-discipline is not legalism—it is faith. When we obey the Word of God, we are living by faith, even when we discipline our lives to accomplish biblical objectives.

Our "daily faith" will cause our "seed faith" to grow into "mountain-moving faith." The question is always asked, "How can we become strong in faith?" Andrew Murray said we can grow "a day's portion every day." God gives us faith each day. We must gather it, feed upon it, and grow in the faith we have. We cannot grow today on next year's faith. Nor can we grow today on last year's lesson. When Israel wandered for forty years in the wilderness, God commanded them, "Behold, I will rain bread from heaven for you; and the people shall go out and gather a certain rate every day, that I may prove them, whether they will walk in my law, or no" (Exodus 16:4).

Just as a little boy must eat daily to grow into a strong man, so we are supplied "daily faith" to grow into a man or woman of God. Just as a small sprout becomes a tree, as a building rises upon its foundation, and as the longest journey begins with a step, so we must develop faith, one step at a time, one day at a time, "one-page-a-day."

One summer I vacationed on Tybee Island off the coast of Georgia. There is a thirteen-mile causeway from the mainland across some smaller islands out to Tybee Island. Workmen were resurfacing the highway when we went out on Monday. Their asphalt laying machine was not traveling more than one mile an hour. I commented to my wife, "It'll take them all summer to pave this road." Returning on Friday, we found both sides of the thirteen-mile causeway resurfaced, in less than a week. Small, but consistent, unnoticed progress is the secret to accomplishing major projects and to becoming a person of faith.

Some have imagined that by great exertion of faith they can move mighty mountains. Perhaps some could kill a Goliath in one attempt, but David had practiced using his sling. He had already killed a lion and a bear. If we can trust God for food, at least breakfast, then we have learned to trust him for greater provisions. If a student can trust God to help him retain his lessons today, eventually he can become a great scholar. Remember, we never become a scholar overnight, nor do we become a champion weight lifter overnight—even to lift mountains by faith.

It would not surprise us if our strength failed because we did not eat or exercise all month. Should it surprise us when we are weak in faith because we did not search the Scriptures or intercede with God? Jesus reminded us, "Man shall not live by bread alone, but by every word that proceedeth out of the mouth of God" (Matthew 4:4). Just as we complain when our stomachs are empty, so we mourn when our faith is weak. The fact that we are concerned about our spiritual weakness shows that we should do something about our faith.

The Crucible Law. All quality products are tested to prove their worth, so victorious faith must be proved in the heat of trials. This temptation or testing is not to destroy our faith. Many wish to have great faith, others pray for it, but only a few attain it, because they flunk the lessons in the school where faith is taught.

If we pray for great faith, first of all, God will try us. The Canaanite woman had a daughter possessed by a devil (Matthew 15:21-23). Surely this was her trial, her thorn in the flesh. Other people have different kinds of trials such as health, money, or opposition from someone. But they will be trials to cause our faith to grow, because trials drive us to Jesus Christ, and there we find faith. Someone said, "Trials are the messengers of God to teach us more faith."

The Lord Jesus did not immediately answer the Canaanite woman's request to deliver her daughter. She prayed fervently, but the Lord seemed to ignore her. Some people come seeking for more faith, but Jesus apparently turns a deaf ear to them. They want to trust him for great things, but to them he is apparently looking the other way.

Perhaps Jesus wants to test them to determine their sincerity, to see whether they will act upon his Word or search for answers in his Word. A faith that still searches for the Lord in spite of silence from heaven is faith upon which we can grow.

The Canaanite woman had to learn humility. She persisted so long that the disciples wanted to send her away. Jesus explained to her, "It is not meet to take the children's bread, and to cast it to dogs" (Matthew 15:26). Jesus explained to her the Old Testament principle, that she was a Gentile and God's plan was for the Jews. She did not give up, but cried, "Yet the dogs eat of the crumbs which fall from their master's table" (Matthew 15:27).

When we look for faith, we must realize that we deserve nothing. The woman realized she was a Gentile; she likened herself to the dogs (a name Jews used for Gentiles), searching for scraps. So, if we look for faith, we must realize we are wretched and sinful. When we arrive at the root of our problem, we have a foundation on which to build. The deeper our realization of the root of our problem, the deeper our humility, and the stronger our faith in God.

The "Faith Up-Front" Law. If we want to get answers to our prayer by faith, we must begin by faith—not wait until God gives us "earnest money faith." All Christians have the Word of God, so we all have an embryonic seed of faith. When God puts us through the crucible of testing, he wants to make sure we trust him. Therefore, before we pray, faith must be active. Before we read the Word, faith must be present. Faith gives perspective to all we do.

The Bible teaches that certain things can be seen with the eyes of faith, not with the physical eyes. This is why faith must be our negotiation with God. Jesus told Martha at the tomb of Lazarus, "Said I not unto thee, that if thou wouldest believe, thou shouldest see the glory of God?" (John 11:40). For Martha to get what she wanted she had first to believe. But the average person has difficulty with God's plan which is "Believing is seeing." The American edict "Seeing is believing" denies New Testament faith.

When Jesus said to the men, "Take ye away the stone" (John 11:39), they did not want to believe him. They reminded Jesus, "He stinketh." That was a statement of unbelief. Jesus wanted them to believe so they could see the miracle.

Faith is the priority for spiritual life. When the unsaved believe in Jesus Christ, they see him perform the miracle of new birth in their lives. We hear Jesus' exhortation to Thomas, "Blessed are they that have not seen, and yet have believed" (John 20:29). Peter repeated the same truth, "Though now ye see him not, yet believing, ye rejoice with joy unspeakable" (1 Peter 1:8).

The Expectancy Law. Jesus Christ promised, "Ask and ye shall receive" (Matthew 7:7), and "If ye shall ask any thing in my name, I will do it" (John 14:14). Faith is taking God at his Word and expecting him to do what he promised. James reminded us, "Let him ask in faith" (James 1:6).

Faith is knowing we will get an answer before we ask. When I was a little boy, I went downtown to the theater almost every Saturday to see my favorite cowboy or spy movie. My dad got paid early on Saturday morning and I went by his store to get money for the movies. I always waited for him at the cash register and asked, "Can I have a quarter for the movies?"

I remember my father digging into his pocket and pulling out a handful of change. Then he would select a quarter and hold it out to me.

It was about four miles from home to where my father worked. I never remember doubting if I would get the money, and I never remember him saying no. Someone once asked, "Did you ever ask for more?" No. I knew what I wanted and he always gave me what I asked. I never asked for more than a quarter. As an earthly boy has faith in his father before he asks, so we should have faith in our heavenly Father to give us our request.

The Impossible Expectation Law. We may experience an implied frustration as we read the New Testament. God expects us to be perfect (Matthew 5:48), yet all of us are sinners. God expects us to love him with all of our hearts (Matthew 22:37), but who can love that deeply? God expects us to walk above sin (1 John 1:7), but we all have sin natures. God expects us not to look upon a woman to lust (Matthew 5:20), but who has a perfect mind?

And then we experience further frustration as we see the example of Jesus Christ. His casual life is much higher than our concerted effort to do good. Not only did he not sin (2 Corinthians 5:21), Jesus Christ went about doing good. He gave himself sacrificially for the world. Frustration comes when we are expected to follow his steps (1 Peter 2:21).

Our senses are shocked when we read the New Testament because we know that we cannot live up to the standard. So what are we to do? Do we collapse in frustration and give up? No! We look for a power outside ourselves to fulfill these expectations. We look for the help of God to live the Christian life. Since God required such a high standard, it is only natural that we expect his help to attain the standard.

God's high standard for us includes an abundant life. Jesus said if we come to him and drink, we will have "rivers of living water flowing out of our innermost being" (John 7:38). He promised his followers "life more abundantly" (John 10:10), but everywhere Christians are defeated, dragging around from day to day. In a sense of self-loathing, they beat themselves because of guilt.

Why does Jesus Christ make such high demands on Christians? He bids us to soar with the eagles, yet we have no wings. He bids us to run with the fastest of animals, yet we have difficulty crawling. Jesus Christ promises he can do "abundantly, above all we could ask or think" (Ephesians 3:20). Why does the Savior lift our expectations? Why does he put standards for us on the supernatural plane?

Some say, "Just so we can see our sinfulness." If that is correct, then we cry out, "Woe is me, for I am undone."

Some say, "To make us fanatics." If that is correct, then all God has is frustrated fanatics. We know what to do, but we cannot attain.

Perhaps we need to see that by the law we can accomplish nothing, but in Christ there is life. The answer is more than following the example of Christ, which is veiled legalism. We must live by the power of Christ and allow him to live through us. If we are to live for Christ, we must partake in the life of Christ. The writer of Hebrews tells us, "For we are made partakers of Christ" (Hebrews 3:14).

Those things that are impossible to the imitators of Christ become natural for those who have the life of Christ in their hearts. In the old life we try to act like Christians. In our new life we have the power of Christ flowing through us. In the old life we tried to stop cheating and lying. In the new life Jesus lives through us. Without Jesus we can do nothing, but we "can do all things through Christ which strengtheneth [us]" (Philippians 4:13).

Those who keep the law find that they are under the condemnation of the law. Paul wrote: "For the law of the Spirit of life in Christ Jesus hath made me free from the law of sin and death" (Romans 8:2). Under the law we were bound for condemnation, but in Jesus Christ there is no condemnation. We have salvation because we have the Savior. We need to move from the flesh life to the Spirit life. The flesh is under the demands of the law of sin. The new man is under the law of Jesus Christ or, as the Bible describes it, the law of faith.

When a rocket is thrust toward the moon, it has to free itself from the law of gravity. When it enters space, it finds itself under a new law. So the defeated man is under the law of sin, which is like the law of gravity. But when he is saved, he enters into the gravity field of a new force. The Christian is under the influence of the new law of Jesus Christ. Therefore, he should live by faith, which is the law of faith (Romans 3:27).

The Gratitude Law. We cannot have the conditions that cause faith without also possessing its results—thanksgiving. Paul reminded us, "So walk ye in him . . . established in the faith, . . . abounding . . . with thanksgiving" (Colossians 2:6, 7). Faith and thanksgiving belong to one another and keep one another in focus. The more we trust in God, the more thankful we shall be for his blessings. And the more we thank God for his blessings, the stronger our faith becomes. When men lack faith, they are usually ungrateful to God. Ingratitude weakens faith.

Why does thanksgiving cause faith to be strengthened? Faith grows when the believing soul wholly forgets himself and turns all his energies over to God. When we look to Jesus Christ without reservations, we are expressing the precise nature of thanksgiving, being entirely occupied with God.

When we examine our unbelief, we see our lack of love, our insincerity, our weaknesses and our sin. When we examine our faith, we are aware that God has been faithful, that he is love, holiness, and goodness. When we realize God has given us the gift of faith, we become thankful for his compassion to us.

If we are seeking to build our faith, we can begin by thanking God. First, we should thank him for the gift of his Son, Jesus Christ, given for sinners. Then we should thank God for the gracious promise of eternal life. We should thank him for his guidance and protection in our lives. Even in failure and defeat, thank God that he is our Lord. We should confess before him that God is great and good. This thanksgiving will teach our souls to trust calmly in God. By rendering thanks to God, we revive our souls and strengthen our faith. And by doing this, we praise God. And in the final analysis, praising God and believing God are one.

CONCLUSION

The Bible never challenges angels to live by faith. They are fixed in their moral relationship to God. They do not have freedom to make decisions, so they cannot have faith. They do not struggle with a sin nature, therefore they cannot have victory. Also, they cannot overcome the adversities and trials of life, so they cannot walk by faith. The angels have a lofty position from which they give glory to God. But man has a far superior potential, for he can overcome his inadequacies. He can do all things through Christ which strengthens him (Philippians 4:13). Man can do the greatest feat possible—he can live by faith.

FIVE
JUSTIFICATION BY FAITH

Faith is believing the unreasonable, the impossible, and the unexplainable, because someone else, in whom we have absolute confidence, has said it was so, and upon his word we believe it, without asking any further proof.
M. R. DeHaan

Some have felt Say-It-Faith is just psyching up oneself or the power of positive thinking. But that is not true. Say-It-Faith is based on a complete understanding of the biblical doctrine of faith.

Before we can move mountains by faith, we must understand that we are justified by faith. "Therefore being justified by faith, we have peace with God through our Lord Jesus Christ" (Romans 5:1). We must understand that our record in heaven is perfect and that God has declared that we are as righteous as Jesus Christ. Then, with all the confidence of heaven, we can say what we want from God and receive it.

Martin Luther, a Catholic priest, searched for God with all his heart but could not find peace. He sincerely followed the teaching and practice of his church but could not find salvation. Finally, Luther was saved when he realized it was not his good works but the righteousness of Jesus Christ that saved anyone. When Luther accepted the truth of "justification by faith," he found the peace he sought. Because of his understanding of justification by faith, he repudiated the Roman Catholic Church.

Night and day I pondered until I saw the connection between the justice of God and the statement "the just shall live by faith." Then I grasped that the justice of God is that righteousness by which through grace and sheer mercy, God justifies us through faith. Thereupon I felt myself to be reborn and to have gone through open doors into paradise.[1]

The continued influence of Luther can be found from that date forward, but nowhere more evident than in the conversion of John and Charles Wesley. A friend of these two young men, William Holland, wrote in his diary that on May 17, 1738, he was "providentially directed to Martin Luther's *Commentary on the Epistle to the Galatians*."[2] He shared his finding first with Charles Wesley.

I carried it round to Mr. Charles Wesley, who was sick at Mr. Bray's, as a very precious treasure that I had found, and we three sat down together, Mr. Charles Wesley reading the Preface aloud. At the words, "What, have we then nothing to do? No, nothing! but only accept Him who of God is made unto us wisdom and righteousness and sanctification and redemption," there came such a power over me as I cannot well describe; my great burden fell off in an instant; my heart was so filled with peace and love that I burst into tears. . . . My companions, perceiving me so affected, fell on their knees and prayed. When I afterwards went into the street, I could scarcely feel the ground I trod upon.[3]

Four days later, Charles Wesley was also converted because of his insight into justification by faith that he read in Martin Luther.

> *I spent some hours this evening in private with Martin Luther, who was greatly blessed to me, especially the conclusion of the second chapter. I laboured, waited and prayed to feel "who loved me, and gave Himself for me."*[4]

Three days later John Wesley was converted when he went to Aldersgate and heard someone read from the *Introduction to Romans*, by Martin Luther. Once again the truth of justification by faith gripped a seeking soul. John Wesley had performed works for salvation, he had fasted, preached, studied, and prayed all night. Yet in his heart he had not experienced the new birth. His diary entry tells of his conversion.

> *In the evening I went very unwillingly to a society in Aldersgate Street, where one was reading Luther's Preface to the Epistle to the Romans. About a quarter before nine, while he was describing the change which God works in the heart through faith in Christ, I felt my heart strangely warmed. I felt I did trust in Christ, Christ alone for salvation; and an assurance was given me that He had taken away my sins, even mine, and saved me from the law of sin and death. (May 24, 1738)*

Just as these people were transformed through proper understanding of justification by faith, so we can enter into peace with God by justification through faith (Romans 5:1).

Abraham is the first person in the Bible described as having been justified by faith. This is not saying he was the first person to be a child of God. "He [Abraham] believed in the Lord; and he [God] counted it to him [Abraham] for righteousness" (Genesis 15:6). God made a promise to Abraham which he accepted as possible and trusted in God as though it were actual. The "believing" by Abraham constituted an act of declaration. In return, God made his declaration.

The Bible testifies of Abraham, "He staggered not at the promise of God through unbelief; but was strong in faith, giving glory to God; and being fully persuaded that, what he had promised, he was able also to perform" (Romans 4:20, 21). The secret to Abraham's faith was his conviction that God would do what he promised.

Once there was a man who wanted a million dollars for a project. The project was his own conception, even though the man wanted to do it for God. The man had not advertised to the public, nor begun the project. It existed only in his mind. He prayed for one million dollars. When God did not send the money, he blamed God.

Yet the man had no right to blame God. The man's faith was based on his dream, not on the Word of God. The secret to Abraham's faith is that he believed God was able also to perform what he had promised.

God promised that Abraham would have a son. This seemed an impossible promise to fulfill. Abraham's wife was beyond childbearing age. Abraham, "considered not his own body now dead" (Romans 4:19). He trusted the promise of God that he would have a son. Therefore, the Bible goes on to say that Abraham "believed, even God, who quickeneth the dead" (Romans 4:17).

If we want more faith, the first step is not to seek faith. We should look beyond faith to its object—God. We must understand the commands and promises of the Bible. Then when we understand what God has promised, we can claim them. Faith is simply accepting what God has promised in his Bible.

As Abraham did not regard his own body, which was already dead, so we must realize that we are dead, dead with Christ. But, further, we must believe that God has given us life and act upon it. God who makes the dead to live, will also give us life that we may serve him.

Justification and righteousness are linked in Scripture, in that both come from the same Greek work (*dikaios* means "righteousness" and *dikaioo* means "to justify"). When we express saving faith in God, God adds righteousness and perfection to our record in heaven. This is the act of justification. Since justification and righteousness represent words of common origin, these can be distinguished by noting that God is the source, making righteous, and man is the recipient, being made righteous.

A double transference happens at salvation. Our sin is transferred to Jesus Christ, and he becomes our sin, taking our punishment. The preposition *for* is the key word, indicating Christ died for us (Galatians 2:20), he gave his life a ransom for many (Matthew 20:20). He gave himself for the sins of the world. The second step of transference is the perfection of Jesus Christ which is credited to our account. When God looks at us in judgment, he sees the perfection of his Son. "For God hath made him to be sin for us [the first step of transference], that we might be made the righteousness of God in him [second step of transference]" (2 Corinthians 5:21).

If we speed on the highway and are arrested, we stand guilty before the law. When we pay for the fine, we go free. However, the state's computer records show that we have a "moving violation" and our insurance rate will probably go up. But, should the judge dismiss the case against us, we are not guilty. Our record has no mark or violation against it. "Acquittal" means the record appears as if the crime never happened. Justification is not the same as acquittal. Justification goes farther than pardon or acquittal. Justification declares that we are perfect drivers or the safest drivers in the state. The record of the best driver in the state is credited to us in the computer. If the governor presents us with a trophy for being the safest drivers in the state, we know we do not deserve it. Other people know we have been caught speeding. But the record shows we are perfect. This same type of action happens when we are justified by faith. We are clothed in the righteousness of Jesus Christ; we are just as perfect as

God's Son. We know we sin and we have lied (Psalm 116:11), yet our record in heaven is perfect.

The state of justification is a legal standing in which the Christian enjoys his life and his blessings (Romans 5:1-11). He no longer has to worry about offending God. He has peace with God because of justification. He realizes at every moment that God has graciously accepted him into his family. By faith he "acts on" the account that is settled in heaven.

Justification is an act whereby our legal position in heaven is changed. Being justified is similar to the act whereby a government declares that an alien is a citizen. The moment the person is pronounced a citizen, nothing happens to him internally. His thought processes remain the same, as does his personality and his pattern of speech. The only actual change is his legal standing. But as he becomes aware of the benefits of being a citizen, he may shout, cry, or break out into a grin. The emotional reaction has no organic connection to his changed legal status, but surely has a connection with his new advantages of being a citizen of a chosen country. In the same way, justification changes our legal papers in heaven. We become a child of God. In response to this new relationship we may cry, rejoice or sit in silent gratitude.

The statement that Abraham, "believed in the Lord; and he counted it to him for righteousness" (Genesis 15:6) gives only one side of the picture of Abraham's faith. Abraham was the "friend of God" (James 2:23) because he walked with God. James seems to say that Abraham was justified by faith because he kept the law (2:23). At this apparent conflict, we must examine the cause and effect relationship of justification by faith.

Justification is the act whereby God declares a person righteous when that person accepts God's Word. Hence, justification teaches that a relationship between God and man can exist. Because of this non-experiential relationship which takes place in heaven a person receives a new

nature. Justification makes man perfect in God's sight—
this is non-experiential and is a man's position in heaven.
On earth, man's new nature struggles with the old desires
of the flesh. In heaven he has been accepted by the
perfection of Jesus Christ, hence no works are necessary.

On earth he must work out his own salvation. On the
earthly level James reminded that "by works a man is
justified, and not by faith only" (James 2:24). These are
two aspects of one truth. Paul taught that justification by
faith is wholly apart from any works.

James taught that justification by works is the outward
evidence that a saved man demonstrates. Paul described
what God sees, and James described what man sees.

Paul looked to the fact that Abraham was justified by
faith (Genesis 15:6). James saw that Abraham in
obedience took his son to Mount Moriah (Genesis
22:1, 19).

Both men spoke of faith. Paul's faith was the cause that
brings about salvation. James' faith was the effect after one
has salvation. "The just shall live by his faith" (Habakkuk
2:4). This is more than accepting salvation. This is
accepting the Lord who declares us righteous, by having
the righteous God live in our life. The Septuagint
translates the verse, "The righteous will live by my
faithfulness (*ek pisteos mou*)." This means that God's
character becomes the means by which a man lives,
because God lives in and through the man. Faith in God
becomes an extension of the major attributes of God,
which is his faithfulness. Hence, *imputed faith* which is
non-experiential, becomes the basis of indwelling faith.

The next chapter describes how the faith of Jesus Christ
is transferred to believers, so that they can testify with
Paul, "Christ liveth in me: and the life which I now live in
the flesh, I live by the faith of the Son of God, who loved
me, and gave himself for me" (Galatians 2:20).

Justification by faith is absolutely necessary for salvation,
but there is more to salvation than justification by faith.

When God justifies us, he takes care of the legal indictment against us because of sin. James said that we must go beyond justification by faith and go to faith by works. He gave the analogy, "For as the body without the spirit is dead, so faith without works is dead also" (James 2:26). He meant that a person can have a physical body, yet that body can be dead. So a man can be justified by faith, yet that person needs a new nature. He needs new life in the body. Life comes when we are born again. With it we get a new nature, new desires; we become a new person (2 Corinthians 5:17).

How can we tell that this body has life? The same way we tell if anyone has life. If one is able to walk—such as walking by faith (2 Corinthians 5:7)—then we say that person has life. Also if a person is able to eat—such as eating the Word of God (John 6:54)—or to drink of the Lord (John 4:14), that person has life.

Perhaps the best way to tie together a man's legal position in heaven and his daily walk on earth is by accepting and applying the truth of Habakkuk 2:4; "The just shall live by his faith." This was the verse that changed Martin Luther's life. As Luther climbed steps in Rome as an act of religious penitence, this was the verse that came to his mind. He stood, in symbolic repudiation of Rome's legal requirement for salvation. He accepted the truth of justification by faith and rested in the salvation provided by Jesus Christ. But that did not stop him from serving his Lord. For the rest of his life, Luther diligently served Jesus Christ. He attempted to harmonize salvation by faith and service by faith.

SIX
INDWELLING FAITH

Faith is the spiritual faculty of the soul which deals with the spiritual realities of the future and the unseen.
Andrew Murray

Say-It-Faith is a subjective confidence of the heart that must be based on objective interpretation of Scripture. In the same manner, the indwelling reality of Jesus Christ is manifested in subjective feelings but is based on the teachings of the Bible.

Those who say what they want God to do for them must be sure that Christ dwells in their hearts, and is allowed to flow out through them. The basis for the indwelling life is realizing we have been crucified with Christ and that his resurrected life will empower us to move mountains when we exercise Say-It-Faith.

On Easter Sunday, 1951, I experienced a special communion with God that I had not previously felt. This sense of Christ's presence has remained with me. I was waiting for my ride to Sunday school. At the time I was teaching in a small Presbyterian mission called Capital View Community Chapel outside Columbia, South Carolina. My ride was approximately thirty minutes late that morning. During that time I meditated on the meaning of Galatians 2:20, especially the "Christ liveth in me" section.

It was the first Easter following my salvation. The phrase "I live by the faith of the Son of God" was a challenge. I realized for the first time that Christ rose on the first Easter and lived in my heart. I experienced his fullness and for the first time I experienced his faith within me. As I stood in the warm sun waiting for my ride, I volitionally yielded my defeated faith to God. I asked Jesus Christ to give me victory by living his faith through me. Jesus Christ had never gotten discouraged, and I wanted faith that could trust God not only for money, but also faith that would not worry about anything. I wanted to trust completely in God.

What I experienced was inward reality. I did not kneel in prayer nor did I close my eyes. I simply talked to Jesus and yielded everything to him. I asked Jesus Christ to live his life through me. That morning for the first time in my Christian life I fully experienced the meaning of the resurrection life. The previous year, when I was still unsaved, Easter had been simply a historical fact. Now I had come to know personally the One who was raised from the dead; and he was not just at the right hand of God in heaven. Christ was alive in my heart. Little did I know that the inner presence of Jesus Christ in me would be tested. But that morning I did not have a care in the world, because I had the faith of Christ.

Later, Dr. R. C. McQuilkin, president of the college, explained in a class that he too had sought victory that comes by Jesus Christ. He explained that each year he went to a youth conference and got his spiritual bucket filled, but during the ensuing months the bucket went dry. Then one year he completely surrendered to Jesus Christ and accepted the Word of God by faith and "sank a well of his own." I had experienced what Dr. McQuilkin and thousands of others experienced. Jesus promised, "Whosoever drinketh of the water that I shall give him shall never thirst; but the water that I shall give him shall be in him a well of water springing up into everlasting life" (John 4:14).

BIBLICAL TEACHING ON INDWELLING

Indwelling faith was the challenge of Jesus to the perplexed disciples. They did not know how to explain the power of God. Jesus told them, "Have faith in God" (Mark 11:22). The King James Version's translation of this verse obscures what Jesus might have been giving them. Jesus said, *"Ekete pistin theou"* which could be translated "Have (the) faith of God." The secret of spiritual power was not their faith but the faith of God in them—indwelling faith.

One of the foundational verses in the Old Testament for faith is "The just shall live by his faith" (Habakkuk 2:4). Note this faith refers to God's faith, not men's faith. God is faithful to enable his children to live for him.

Indwelling faith is someone else's faith at work for us. We cease all efforts to please God, we give up even our natural faith, and let the faith of the Son of God work for us. Paul noted, "Knowing that a man is not justified by the works of the law, but by the faith of Jesus Christ" (Galatians 2:16). This means that the faith of Jesus Christ must be planted in our hearts—that is, the indwelling faith. Later in the same chapter Paul repeats the same point but applies this implantation to sanctifying faith, "I live by the faith of the Son of God who loved me and gave himself for me" (Galatians 2:20). The apostle is teaching that success in his Christian life was the result of the faith of Jesus Christ.

Therefore, faith does not spring from our hearts. Faith is not even natural faith helped along or dressed up for God. Faith is not even our natural faith with a new object. Biblical faith is the indwelling of *Christ's faith* in our hearts.

Some authorities have questioned whether the phrase "the faith of Christ" should be translated that way. They interpret the original language *pisteos Iesou Christou* to be an objective genitive, meaning "through faith in Jesus Christ." Those who would translate it this way make it our faith in Christ, implying that he is the object of faith. But other authorities translate the phrase "the faith of Christ" as a subjective genitive, making the faith that belongs to Jesus Christ.

Actually, scholars translate the phrase in light of Paul's Hebrew background. They translate *pisteos* to mean "The faithfulness of Jesus Christ." Meaning, when we come to the phrase *pisteos Iesou Christou,* we are not describing Jesus' faith but we are describing the faithfulness of Jesus.[1] In the Old Testament the word *emunah* meant both faithfulness and faith. In the New Testament the word *pistis* can also mean faithfulness and faith.

Sinners are saved through the faithfulness of Jesus Christ, that is, "the righteousness of God [is manifested through the faithfulness] of Jesus Christ to all who believe" (Romans 3:22, my paraphrase; see KJV). Because Jesus Christ was faithful in his life, and was faithful to death, then God's righteousness is revealed to us. The same impact is seen in Galatians 2:16, "Knowing that a man is not justified by the works of the law, but by the [faithfulness] of Jesus Christ, even we have believed in Jesus Christ in order to be justified on the basis of the [faithfulness] of Christ" (my paraphrase; see KJV).

We are justified by faith because Jesus Christ was a faithful sacrifice for our sins. "The scripture hath concluded all under sin, that the promise [which is based upon the faithfulness] of Jesus Christ might be given to them who believe" (Galatians 3:22, my paraphrase; see KJV). Jesus Christ was faithful to fulfill all the promises in the Old Testament, so that we can believe in him today. Again Paul says that salvation is based on this concept. "Not having mine own righteousness, which is of the law, but that which is through the [faithfulness] of Christ, the righteousness of God which is by faith" (Philippians 3:9, my paraphrase; see KJV). In this verse we are not saved by our good works or our faithfulness, but we are saved through the faithfulness of Jesus Christ. All of salvation depends upon him. Therefore, we can pray and approach the throne because of the faithfulness of Christ. "In whom we have boldness and access with confidence [through his faithfulness]" (Ephesians 3:12, my translation; see KJV).

Thus we have faith because of Jesus Christ who was faithful in all things. And since "faithful" grows out of "faith," we say that Jesus Christ has faith. T. F. Torrance has explained,

Jesus Christ is thus not only the incarnation of the divine pistis, *but He is the embodiment and actualization of man's* pistis *in covenant with God. He is not only the righteousness of God, but the embodiment and actualization of our human righteousness before God.*[2]

Another aspect of the faith of Jesus Christ is the admonition of Paul. "If . . . we were reconciled to God by the death of his Son, much more . . . we shall be saved by his life" (Romans 5:10). The phrase "his life" refers to much more than the resurrection life of Jesus Christ. It also refers to his earthly life of obedience, his risen life of ministering to the disciples after his resurrection, of standing in heaven as the seal of our faith before God. Inasmuch as the entire life of Jesus Christ is an assurance of our salvation, that surely includes his faith. That means his indwelling faith is the basis of our expression of faith.

Certain rights are available to Americans because of their citizenship. They can vote, hold office, express opinions and, of course, have the protection of the Constitution which guarantees their right to life, liberty, and the pursuit of happiness. In the same manner, if one is a Christian, there are certain rights available to him. He can have victory over sin, get his prayers answered, walk in peace, and enjoy holiness and communion with God.

A foreigner can never enjoy the benefits of being American without having become an American citizen. A sinner can never enjoy the benefits of a Christian life without being born again as a Christian. Jesus told Nicodemus, "Ye must be born again" (John 3:7). When Christ took us to the cross where he died, he also took us down into the grave and brought us forth a "new creation" from the grave. In essence we were given life through the grave. The old nature was judged on the cross; a new nature was imparted to us through the resurrection. His death and resurrection allows us to be born again into new life.

Some who were not born Americans became U. S. citizens by naturalization. They were not born Americans but later in life took an oath and became American citizens. How a person becomes a Christian can be pictured two ways. Christians become citizens of the kingdom of God, as we have described. We also see that Christians are those who are adopted into the family of God. Adoption pictures how we became God's legal children. Adoption is not something we experience but is a legal transaction which takes place in heaven by which we legally become God's children.

However, many Americans do not enjoy all the privileges of American citizenship. Some act like slaves or criminals because of their ignorance or because of neglect. Certain Americans are starving while others feast. The fact of being an American does not solve all a person's problems. If he does not take advantage of his citizenship, it is his fault. In the same way, many Christians are not taking advantage of their heavenly citizenship. They allow Satan to defeat them or they give in to the flesh. They are miserable and defeated. Having Christ in their lives should give them victory, but they are defeated. Victory depends upon taking advantage of the crucified life available to them.

INDWELLING BASED ON THE CROSS

How can we take advantage of the crucified life? On the basis of the cross, we must recognize our oneness with Jesus Christ in death, burial, and resurrection. In Christ we are new persons. We were grafted into a new tree; we belong to Jesus Christ. We became partners of a new corporation; we belong to the kingdom of God. Now we must take advantage of the divine life that flows from the cross of Jesus Christ to us.

There comes a time when we need a new look at the redemptive work of Jesus Christ. Our blind eyes must be opened to the renewed meaning of the cross of Jesus Christ. We humbly bow before Jesus Christ, lift up our eyes and the cross is revealed before us. We see Christ as the divine sin-bearer. We ask ourselves, "Why have I not seen him before?" The answer comes back, "The loathsome thing called self has blinded your eyes."

We need to see again that Jesus died unto sin. And his death is the basis of victory over the domination of our "self-life." We do not need a new work of grace, or a "second work of grace." We need to go back to Calvary and reckon ourselves dead (Romans 6:11) with Christ on the cross.

Our sinful selves were put to death positionally (Romans 6:6), but they usually remain active in our lives (Romans 7:15-23). What we need to do is sign the death sentence to our self-life and not give it the authority to control us (Romans 6:13). We need to realize that Christ not only died for us as sinners, but that we, as sinners, potentially died in Jesus Christ. That means our old natures were put to death, but also it means we were given new natures. We can now have victory over sin because we have powerful new natures (Ephesians 4:24), indwelt by the Holy Spirit, that have the potential to give us victory.

Our victory is in our participation in the crucifixion life. We are brought again to Calvary where we realize that we died with him. The cross signified pain, shame, ignominy, and death. That is why the cross saves. It separates all that is past from all that God wants to do for us. The cross is not divine magic. The cross is the life of Christ being substituted for our sin. The cross is the life of Christ being transferred. The cross is the life of Jesus Christ being planted in our place. Our sin in Christ and his life in us is the greatest transfer in life (2 Corinthians 5:21).

It is folly to talk about any type of spiritual victory apart from our participation in the cross of Jesus Christ. Too many times Christians have tried to be saved by the cross, but continue to live by self-effort. But all victory begins when we renounce the "old life" and lay hold of the "new life" which we get by identification with Jesus Christ.

To have victory, we must realize that the Bible teaches, "the flesh profiteth nothing" and "our old man is crucified with Christ" and "they that are Christ's have crucified the flesh with the affections and lusts."

Victory over the world is reckoning ourselves to be dead to sin (Romans 6:11). We are defeated because we have allowed "the flesh, the world, and the devil" (1 John 2:16) to overcome us. We know that even by imitating the Lord we cannot have victory over the flesh. We must go beyond acting like the Lord, for that never conquers sin; we must allow him to indwell us. The fact that he gave himself for us is the secret of victory. Now he lives in our lives and wants to be our victory.

The key to victory is a moment-by-moment dependence on Jesus Christ. If we surrender our desires to him, we no longer agonize over the temptation. We do not strive against the flesh to overcome it. We let the victory of Jesus Christ overcome the old life. In essence, victory is a good thing; it is a lovely thing. It is like people dancing in the streets after a war. Just as they experience freedom, so when we allow Jesus Christ to rule in our hearts, we allow him the freedom to give us victory over the world.

Too often in seeking victory, we neglect God's teaching

through nature. The laws of nature show how God gives life. Every time spring comes around, we realize that life grows out of death. There is not a tree or plant that has not grown from the death of a seed. First it must be planted in the ground and die. And if it dies, it springs forth into new life. In the same way we see our new life in Jesus Christ. First Jesus Christ had to die for our sins. Then we must learn to die, even as Paul said, "I die daily" (1 Corinthians 15:31).

The Bible teaches that the Christian enjoys life on two planes. First, he lives in this sinful life; he is not perfect but must continually strive against temptation. But in the second plane the Christian lives "in the heavenlies" (Ephesians 1:3). On this plane, the Christian is as perfect as the Son of God. He enjoys all the benefits of the heavenlies.

In the first plane the Christian is limited by his physical body, tempted by his fleshly nature, and subject to the embarrassments of earthly life. On the higher plateau, he is identified with Jesus Christ, he possesses the new life of Christ, and he stands perfect in Christ's righteousness. The Christian on this plane is just as perfect as Jesus Christ. Our first life is our state on this earth; our second life is our standing before God.

When Paul announced to the Ephesians that Jesus has "blessed us with all spiritual blessings in heavenly places in Christ" (Ephesians 1:3), he was telling us that we are rich in heaven, even though we seem poor on this earth. It is not that we have to die physically to receive these blessings; they are our present heritage.

By faith the Christian may sit with Jesus Christ in the heavenlies and enjoy all of the benefits of Calvary. This is not schizophrenia. This does not mean the mind of the Christian dwells in the heavenlies, but his body dwells on earth. God wants us to realize our potential as a basis of overcoming our obstacles. "He that spared not his own Son, but delivered him up for us all, how shall he not with him also freely give us all things?" (Romans 8:32). Someone calls this "the throne life." Even though Christians tread the dust of this earth, they sit upon a heavenly throne.

Some say, "I cannot understand this teaching because it is a mystery." At the heart of every doctrine there is something we do not understand; something we must accept by faith.

The earthly life of Jesus Christ illustrates our resurrection life. While Jesus walked on this earth, he was subject to its limitations. Yet he said, "No man hath ascended up to heaven, but he that came down from heaven, even the Son of man which is in heaven" (John 3:13). As he was talking, Jesus said he existed at that moment in heaven. Here was a miracle that the people could not understand. Jesus was preaching and they saw him with their physical eyes. Yet while he was on earth he spoke of "the Son of man which is in heaven." Since we live in Christ, we can be on earth at the same time that we dwell in the heavenlies.

Most of us know about earthly life but very few know anything about heavenly life. When we live in the heavenlies, we have been set free to do his will. It does not mean we are perfect, nor does it mean that we are without the sinful flesh, nor that our bodies do not get sick, or our businesses fail. We must all die. But our heavenly life means that we apply the power of Jesus Christ to help us overcome spiritual obstacles.

What then, is the life of indwelling faith? We live for Jesus Christ in the fullness that he purchased on Calvary. We live for Jesus Christ as though we were in the heavenlies while we are still on this earth. We take his wealth and pay our spiritual debts. We claim his victory and overcome the emptiness of this life. We let the faith of Jesus Christ dwell in us so that he gets the victory for us.

CONCLUSION

There are two secrets to the victory of indwelling faith. First, we must allow the power of Jesus Christ to flow out through our lives. This is done when we yield to Christ and allow his faith to control our lives.

Second, when we see our perfection in heaven, we conform our walk on this earth to our heavenly position. We walk by faith when we attempt to live our lives on this earth to reflect our perfection in heaven. It takes faith for a Christian to see his relationship to his two walks.

SEVEN
THE GIFT OF FAITH

True faith is the most active motive power in the whole world. "Faith, which worketh by love," works all sorts of marvels; and where there is this true faith, it will prove its reality by its practicalness. Charles Spurgeon

Say-It-Faith is one of the gifts of the Holy Spirit that a Christian uses to serve God. Therefore we must understand the nature of spiritual gifts and how to exercise faith if we want to move mountains. Paul wrote, "And though I have the gift of prophecy, and understand all mysteries, and all knowledge; and though I have all faith, so that I can remove mountains, and have not charity, I am nothing" (1 Corinthians 13:2).

Some people obviously have more faith than others. As we study the Bible, we see some men accomplish tasks by faith. Abraham was one hundred years old, yet miraculously fathered a child. Through faith he overcame the barrenness of Sarah's womb. Could we trust God for a similar miracle?

Moses stood before the multitude and commanded, "Stand still and you shall see it come to pass." By faith he knew that God would roll back the waters of the Red Sea, therefore he exercised the spoken word of faith that we have called Say-It-Faith.

Some might say that it was easy for people in biblical times to have faith. They heard the actual voice of God or they saw his angel. They experienced the miracles of God—why should they not have faith? That person claims we have no supernatural basis for our faith. Yet, he forgets that God still speaks to us through the Scriptures. God will do all that he promised to do. Remember the Bible is the greatest miracle that God has given to us. Just as Christ performed a miracle by healing a blind man, so God performed a miracle in giving us the Bible.

A miracle happens when God transcends the laws of nature with a law that is more powerful. A miracle is a significant event that accomplishes God's purpose and glory. When God revealed the message of the Bible, inspired each word to guarantee accuracy, and preserved it for us—that is a miracle. Just as the disciples believed on Jesus Christ because he supernaturally created wine (John 2:11), so our faith in God is based on the supernatural Word of God.

Charles Hughes, a student at Liberty Baptist Seminary, was a powerful young evangelist who traveled to weekend revivals. In March of 1978, he was involved in a tragic head-on collision on the interstate highway in southern Pennsylvania. For several days he hung precariously between life and death. Because there was so much brain damage, the doctors said that he would be a mere vegetable for the rest of his life.

Finally, one day after Charles had gone through a number of emergency surgeries, the doctors were ready to give up, saying he was clinically dead. They approached his father, Dr. Robert Hughes, regarding permission for his organs to be used as transplants.

"No!" Dr. Hughes said in his meek manner. "God gave me young Charles and he is to preach the gospel . . . I will not give him up." Dr. Hughes believed that God would raise his son to preach the gospel. He exercised Say-It-Faith to the doctors and went in the small hospital chapel to pray.

Jerry Falwell had sponsored young Charles and also expressed Say-It-Faith. While Charles was not expected to live, Falwell announced to the congregation at Thomas Road Baptist Church, "Next year Charles Hughes will preach the graduation sermon for Liberty Baptist College." An extraordinary statement, considering that a seminary student usually does not preach graduation sermons, much less a student expected to die.

One year later, May 1979, Charles Hughes stood before the large audience on Liberty Mountain and delivered a powerful graduation sermon. Both his father, Dr. Robert Hughes, and his pastor, Dr. Jerry Falwell, had expressed Say-It-Faith.

These extraordinary expressions of faith are not usually expressed by the average Christian. Someone replies, "That's more faith than I could have."

The Bible describes the extraordinary gifts given to some people to serve God. These spiritual gifts are a person's ability to accomplish the work of God. In our day, these are usually called "serving gifts." Some of them are described as preaching, teaching, serving or the gift of administration (1 Corinthians 12:8-11, 28-30; Ephesians 4:11; Romans 12:6-8). However, the Bible identifies faith as one of the "serving gifts" given by the Holy Spirit to believers. In identifying the different gifts, Paul included "to another faith by the same Spirit" (1 Corinthians 12:9). Since faith appears in the list of spiritual gifts, it is apparently not a reference to saving faith as in: "For by grace are you saved through faith, and that not of yourselves, it is the gift of God" (Ephesians 2:8, 9).

In another place, Paul listed the gift of faith with the gift of preaching (prophecy): "Having then gifts differing according to the grace given to us, whether prophecy, let us prophesy, according to the proportion of faith"

(Romans 12:6). Some are not sure whether the word "faith" in this verse is used to describe the preacher's belief in God that brings power through his preaching, or whether Paul is saying that faith is a special gift exercised independently of preaching. If faith is separate from preaching, it means that a person could serve God by trusting him to supply money for buildings, or trusting God for results during a soul-winning campaign.

Again, Paul used the gift of faith to illustrate love: "And though I have the gift of prophecy, and understand all mysteries, and all knowledge; and though I have all faith, so that I can remove mountains, and have not charity, I am nothing" (1 Corinthians 13:2). The gift of faith is listed with the gift of prophecy, giving the ability of faith equal status with the ability to preach. The one who "moves the mountain of unbelief" is just as important as the one who preaches for the revival. In actuality, one gift such as faith is involved with another gift such as preaching, but we have separated them to examine the nature of faith. When Paul said "all faith" (1 Corinthians 13:2), he probably included more than a reference to the six different expressions of faith. "All" probably includes the object of faith (faith and its object cannot be separated), so Paul was saying that; if all barriers were removed by faith and all things could be accomplished by faith, the results are nothing without love.

Since 1 Corinthians 12 was written to explain to Christians their spiritual gifts, we can only conclude that faith is a special ability given to some people to serve God. I have often said that Jerry Falwell has more faith than anyone else I know. The basis of this statement is his supernatural gift of faith. Jerry Falwell got his faith from God. But we should not give up because of our lack of faith. The Bible teaches that anyone can grow in whatever gift he has by following God's rules concerning the spiritual gifts. To understand the nature of spiritual gifts, we must understand that there were different kinds of gifts given to different people (1 Corinthians 12:4-6). Paul explained this by stating: "Having then gifts differing according to the grace that is given to us" (Romans 12:6).

Jesus was teaching us about gifts when he gave the parable of the talents. In more than a coincidence, one man was given five talents, the second two talents, and the last man one talent. It is very obvious that the Lord gave a different gift to each man, illustrating the fact that the Lord gives a different number of spiritual gifts to people. It is also not a coincidence that the word *talent* (a weight of precious metal, silver or gold) in the parable actually came to mean in English "abilities." A gifted person is also talented. Actually, a talent, in a parable, was $10,000 if it was silver. If it was a talent of gold it would have been worth over $750,000. The person with one talent might be similar to a new Christian who has only one talent of serving Jesus Christ by cutting grass, sweeping out the classroom buildings, or washing windows in the church. The five-talent Christian is similar to those who teach Sunday school, sing in the choir, have a knowledge of Scripture, are wise in counseling people, and also can administer the vacation Bible school. Everyone has a different number of talents; therefore, some might have the gift of faith, while the next person does not use it.

The spiritual gifts are also qualitative in usefulness, meaning two people might have the same gift, but one person has a greater use of that gift than the second person. As an illustration, some who have the gift of teaching are more effective than others who teach the Word of God. The spiritual gift of teaching is not measured by how many pass or fail a course, but how deeply the lives have been changed. Paul evaluated the effectiveness of a spiritual gift as "the manifestation of the Spirit" (1 Corinthians 12:7). When a spiritual gift is properly exercised, the Holy Spirit will manifest himself in the lives of the hearers through the fruits of the Spirit, such as love, joy, and peace (Galatians 5:22, 23).

Therefore, we understand why some have more results in serving God than others; it is because they have a greater spiritual gift. This is why J. O. Grooms, minister of evangelism at the Thomas Road Baptist Church, is one of the most effective soul-winners in America. I believe he has the gift of faith to trust God that lost souls will get saved. Last year he led over 1200 people to Christ. Not only does he begin each morning at five o'clock praying for lost people, he diligently presents the gospel to lost people in door-to-door visitation and telephone evangelism. He mixes intercessory prayer and diligent work with the gift of faith and, as a result, many are won to Jesus Christ.

So where does that leave us? Since some outstanding men of God have the gift of faith, should we give up? No! But some give up because they think they do not have the gift of faith. They think they cannot trust God to "move mountains." A careful study of spiritual gifts will reveal that God is not partial. What he has done for Jerry Falwell, he can do for us . . . if we are willing to learn the same lessons.

Paul taught that we should "Covet earnestly the best gifts" (1 Corinthians 12:31). This means that we can desire the best gifts that God has to offer. If we feel that preaching is the best gift for us, we should pray and ask God to increase our ability to preach. In another place Paul exhorted, "If any man desire the office of a bishop, he desireth a good work" (1 Timothy 3:1). Therefore, it is only natural that we have dreams of what God can do through us. If we desire to have faith like Paul or Moses, we should rejoice, for faith can come with desire.

But some will say that the gifts are given sovereignly, that God controls both the choice and the gift. Dr. Charles Ryrie, professor of theology at Dallas Theological Seminary, responds, "If God gives you a spiritual gift, he will also give you a desire to use it." Therefore if you have a desire for more faith, it is evident that you probably have the gift of faith in your heart.

If we are children of God, we are saved by faith, and with that salvation we have the faith of God in our hearts. The Bible teaches that Jesus Christ provided for the spiritual gifts at salvation: "When he ascended up on high, he led captivity captive, and gave gifts unto men" (Ephesians 4:8). This reference to the resurrection appears in the center of the passage on spiritual gifts, teaching that spiritual gifts were bestowed to us at the resurrection of Christ. Since all men are not equal in gifts, and men can grow in their gifts, it is apparent that Jesus gave the gifts embryonically. We have in latent form, the gift of faith in our hearts. Now God expects us to exercise our faith, so it will grow.

In the parable of the talents, the man who was given five talents used them wisely. When the lord came back, he was given five other talents, making a total of ten talents. Faithfulness in the use of small gifts leads to a larger sphere of service. The man who faithfully teaches a Sunday school class of small children may be preparing himself to preach in the jails or at a rescue mission service. The person who sacrificially gives his tithes from a small salary is preparing himself to give much larger gifts in the future. "He that giveth, let him do it with simplicity" (Romans 12:8).

We should examine our spiritual gifts. Perhaps we have the gift of faith and are not exercising it properly. Paul exhorted, "Now concerning spiritual gifts, brethren, I would not have you ignorant" (1 Corinthians 12:1). We should not be ignorant of our gifts, nor of what we can do for God. Since the proper use of our spiritual gifts will lead to greater usefulness, we can have a more profitable life for God by faithfully doing the small thing today. And since Christians grow on victories, so we will grow "from faith to faith" (Romans 1:17).

EIGHT
THE STATEMENT OF FAITH

Faith may be a creed, valuable in its way, yet having no living power. Faith may represent something far short of the biblical meaning. But faith in the Bible is always something that reaches through until it touches God; through the smoke of battle, through the murk and misery that appall us, through the darkness of the hour, through the threatening forces of evil that seem so rampant— through, and beyond that, behind that, way above that, to God. Faith is that which reaches Him and touches Him.
G. Campbell Morgan

The Scriptures call doctrine "the faith," implying that effective personal faith must be grounded on correct doctrinal faith. To have Say-It-Faith that moves obstacles, we must purge out false doctrine and study carefully all the doctrines of Scripture. Then we stand on a mountain that is taller and firmer than all the obstacles we want to move out of our lives.

Up until now we have seen personal faith as an action that produces salvation or godliness. But in this chapter faith is an external foundation upon which inner belief is grounded. Previously, faith was described as an experience. In this chapter it is fact, as factual as the doctrinal statement of a church. Earlier, faith was described as subjective, influenced by fluctuation and challenged to grow. But in this chapter faith is objective and unchangeable. In previous chapters, faith has been used as a verb. In this chapter it is a noun preceded by an article and called "the faith."

The Bible identifies "the faith" as the doctrinal statement of Christians. As such, it is their theology, or sometimes called their "confession of faith." Because the phrase "the faith" is the content of Christianity, it is also the substance of salvation that a person believes to be saved.

When Jude exhorted "Ye should earnestly contend for the faith which was once delivered unto the saints" (Jude 3), he was indicating that a person should defend the doctrinal content of Christianity because of its inherent completeness. Nothing can be added to it, nor can anything be taken from it. Paul warned against those who shall "depart from the faith" (1 Timothy 4:1). Later he identified them as having "denied the faith" (1 Timothy 5:8), and those who have "erred from the faith" (1 Timothy 6:10, 21), and those who are "reprobate concerning the faith" (2 Timothy 3:8). In these warnings he was describing the standard of faith—objective faith that changes not. As Paul faced death, he testified, "I have kept the faith" (2 Timothy 4:7), meaning he had not changed his belief or his attitude toward doctrine. It was the content of his faith that motivated him to carry the gospel throughout the Mediterranean world.

Christians are told to "stand fast in the faith" (1 Corinthians 16:13), because the faith is the anchor of their souls (Hebrews 6:19). Paul described it as "the word of faith, which we preach" (Romans 10:8), and exhorted the Colossians to continue living in it (Colossians 1:23).

In another place Paul said he had been striving for the faith of the gospel (Philippians 1:27) and because he had been faithful, God had given him a young man to carry on the propagation and defense of the faith. Paul referred to Timothy as "my own son in the faith" (1 Timothy 1:2).

James used the meaning of "the faith" to apply the Jewish creed of the Old Testament (James 2:14, 26). He described Jewish theology, "Thou believest that God is one" (James 2:19). This was the creedal confession of an orthodox Jew as expressed in the *shema* (Deuteronomy 6:4). The Jews felt this statement of faith in the unity of God was foundational to salvation. Here, James, writing to the Jews, indicated the necessity of orthodoxy, of believing in one God. The phrase "thou believest" while containing a verb, plainly refers to the use of faith as a noun.

What is the relationship between the noun faith and the verb faith? The writer of Hebrews said that when the gospel is preached (the faith—noun) it should be mixed with subjective faith (the verb). "For unto us was the gospel preached, as well as unto them: but the word preached did not profit them, not being mixed with faith in them that heard it" (Hebrews 4:2).

The gospel message was more than content. It was spirit that gave men life and victory. First, the message was given by inspiration of the Holy Spirit (2 Timothy 3:16). Second, the words were indwelt with the Spirit (John 6:63). As a result, when a man mixes the message of God with faith, it produces the life of God in his heart. Since the inspired Word of God is the expression of the incarnate Word of God, they both accomplish the same result. Jesus, the Word of God, gives life (John 1:1; 1:14), and the inspired Word also gives life (Hebrews 4:12; James 1:18; 1 Peter 1:23).

When the object of our faith is the person of Jesus Christ as revealed in the Bible, faith is conceived, given life, and grows. The same can be said of Scripture. As we get the message of salvation in our hearts, it gives us faith. "Faith cometh by hearing and hearing by the word of God" (Romans 10:17). The objective and the subjective faith are linked together. These are not two separate actions. They are identical. We get the faith of the Son of God when we get the Word of God in our hearts.

Subjective faith must be based upon God's objective faith. This body of doctrine is contained in all sixty-six books of the Bible. It takes all the revelation of God to assemble a complete statement of faith. If we leave out one of the books of the Bible, a portion of God's revelation will be missing and we will not have a complete statement of "the faith."

As we look at the Bible, we find that God did not reveal his message in a theological statement called a "confession of faith." God has left this up to Christians to formulate. In the process of time, men have come up with Presbyterian statements of faith, Lutheran statements of faith, and Wesleyan statements of faith. The purpose of this chapter is not to determine which is right or wrong. Rather, there is a core of truth in most of these statements of faith, commonly called the fundamentals of the faith. This embryo of faith is that irreducible statement that must be believed if men are to be saved. Man cannot take away or add to the fundamentals of the faith. This is the objective faith upon which we build our subjective faith.

God did not give us theology in a creedal statement, because men would have approached faith as they study mathematics. If God had spoken in a theological formula, men would have treated it as they do an algebraic formula. God did not want dead orthodoxy or mere memorization of a creed. God wants men to give him their lives and live for him.

When we attempt to determine our faith, we immediately realize that certain words we presently use are not found in the Bible, such as *trinity, rapture,* and other theological words we use today. But the truth of these doctrines is taught in the Bible, so we might ask, how did these words get there? How do we find out what they mean? The final question could have been the first:

How do we arrive at a doctrinal statement of faith since God did not give us one?

First, we must study all the Scriptures. We take one doctrine, such as the doctrine of Christ and try to examine all of the verses that say anything about him to see what God has said on the topic. We must be careful not to "proof text," which means to hang all of our doctrine on one verse or use Scripture to support foregone conclusions. We should look at all the Scriptures to find out what God says about Christ, or the Trinity. After men had examined everything about the godhead they used the word *trinity* because it best explained the Bible teaching of God the Father, God the Son, and God the Holy Spirit.

Second, we must interpret and integrate all the facts. This means we must find out what God says about a doctrine, not what we think about it. In doing this, we should not spend all of our time explaining away difficult verses nor try to make a verse fit our doctrinal statement.

In the third place, we should write a statement that reflects the facts we have studied. Here we compare them and fit them together into a complete statement. We should be careful that we do not spend more time on what we reject than on what we believe. When we study the Bible we should never base one doctrine solely on an isolated text. Many cults have done this and arrived at false doctrines. Our personal faith must be grounded in correct doctrine. We must make sure that all the verses on a topic relate to one another and that all our doctrines are interrelated.

We should place emphasis where the Bible emphasizes content. The Bible says much about sin, salvation, and the Savior. If our personal faith is not concerned with these, we may be sincere in our faith, but sincerely wrong. We must beware of getting caught up on tangents minimized in the Bible.

Good doctrine is directed by God to our intellects. God

rarely violates the rational nature he has given us. God is a rational being and, since we are created in his image, we are also rational beings. Therefore, God will use the channel of reasonable thought to communicate with us. God will not speak gibberish, nor will he make us psychotic or irrational mystics. God's ways go beyond man's reason, simply because the mind of an infinite God goes beyond the mind of finite man. But God will never ask us to believe in a square circle, nor a door with only one side. He may ask us, as he did childless Abraham and Sarah, to believe him for miracles, but he generally deals with us in rational terms.

There are several attitudes we will have to take in studying the Bible. These attitudes will give us direction in how to arrive at our belief in God and other areas of Christian doctrine.

First, we must recognize that the human mind is limited. God says, "My thoughts are not your thoughts, neither are my ways your ways, saith the Lord. For as the heavens are higher than the earth, so are my ways higher than your ways and my thoughts than your thoughts" (Isaiah 55:8, 9).

Second, God has not revealed everything to us. We know the essential things but those things less important he has not made clear. The Bible is silent on some things. Jesus told his disciples, "What I do thou knowest not now; but thou shalt know hereafter" (John 13:7). Therefore, there are certain things about our faith that we will not understand until we get to heaven.

A third area deals with the inadequacy of language. Paul described "unspeakable words," which means our words cannot adequately describe God (2 Corinthians 12:4). Because God is high above men, words can never fully describe him.

Fourth, we do not have all facts that are knowable. Since our knowledge of the Bible is incomplete, we must pray with David, "Open thou mine eyes, that I may behold wondrous things out of thy law" (Psalm 119:18).

The Bible tells us that our understanding is darkened because of sin (2 Corinthians 4:3, 4). This simply means we cannot comprehend everything because our minds are distorted by the sin nature. Unbelief will always be natural for us. Therefore, we must strive for a complete faith that is strong and growing.

Also, we must not rule out the imperfect state of science. Whereas a scientist may say two facts are disconnected, from God's point of view there may be harmony. Remember, at one time scientists taught that only ninety-two chemical elements made up the physical universe. Many years later they said there were 115 elements in the world. And scientists continually find more of what they call "basic elements" from which the world is made. So, if science disagrees with the apparent teachings of the Bible, withhold judgment till all facts are known. We must not let a scientist shake our faith.

When we are trying to find a basis for our faith, flee the basic causes of wrong doctrine. Realize that sin in our lives will produce unbelief (John 5:39, 40). Second, if you have only half-knowledge or ignorance, we will have a rotten foundation for a superstructure of faith. We must watch out that we do not build doctrine on "feelings." If we have too much heart and not enough head, we may reject hell because it seems unloving. Or we may reject the written record of the miracles of Christ because they appear irrational, at least in our minds. Intellectual pride can destroy our faith. Some have corrupted their faith because they tried to make doctrine enjoyable to the unsaved. Some aspects of Christianity are truth, but cannot be made palatable.

The 80s have been called "the decade of doctrine," meaning people are examining the contents of Christianity more than ever before, because the modern academic attainment of mankind is more sophisticated, causing man to question everything and search for answers. Also, the pervasive character of unbelief drives men to search for answers beyond the physical world. Who would have thought a few years ago that modern Americans would turn to the occult, the Eastern religions, and metaphysical phenomena in drugs, mysticism, and other sources.

The beliefs of Christianity are questioned because of the collapse of the established church. Institutional Christianity is drifting from its heritage. At one time the family, business, and even government were outwardly based on alleged Christian principles. Now people are searching for original Christianity. Secular humanism is driving people to evangelical reality. They have not found answers to the ultimate questions in man. People know they do not have the answers within. When they ask their questions, they look without. They are looking to God himself, not traditional religion nor the institutional church. People are searching, not always knowing they are searching for God himself and they will not arrive at personal faith until they arrive at a correct understanding of *the faith*.

NINE
HOW TO GROW FAITH

Faith is my acceptance of God's fact. It always has its foundations in the past. What relates to the future is hope rather than faith, although faith often has its object or goal in the future. Watchman Nee

We should not be discouraged if we consider our faith to be weak. Faith is not inanimate. It can grow. Paul tells us to go "from faith to faith," so we can grow from the beginning—to maturity—Say-It-Faith. This chapter offers practical helps to growing our faith so we can trust God for greater answers to prayer.

Saving faith is not large or small. Either a person has it or he does not. Saving faith is described as faith that cannot grow. Saving faith just exists. Like the atom that is the building block of matter, this faith is the building block of God's spiritual kingdom. Jesus described it, "Except you have faith as a grain of mustard seed" (Matthew 13:31). The mustard seed is one of the smallest particles observable by man. And Jesus likened mustard seeds to faith so small it could hardly be seen. Jesus was saying either we have faith or we do not. To get into

God's kingdom we must have the smallest discernible amount of faith. The smallest measure of faith pleases God and becomes the basis for God to save that person.

The Bible describes a man as "weak in faith" (Romans 4:19) and later declares another person "strong in faith" (Romans 4:20). These two statements demonstrate that we can grow in our faith. Our faith grows because it is *living faith*. Growing faith guides us through the problems of life and helps us live for God.

Paul wrote that we should go from *initial faith* which saves us to *daily faith* by which we live. The apostle described this step as "from faith to faith" (Romans 1:17). The steps of growing faith are simple, yet appear difficult, because they fly in the face of man who wants to be self-dependent.

How do we grow from weak faith to strong faith? We cannot strive for faith nor can we work it up in the flesh. Getting faith is not like a man picking up heavy bundles. In order to do that, he grunts and strains. When we want more faith, we cannot grunt or strain to get more. We cannot work up faith. Faith comes without effort, and sometimes the less energy we expend, the more faith we have. And, at times, we give no "grunt" whatsoever when we have the most faith.

WE GROW IN FAITH THROUGH THE WORD OF GOD

As we make the Word of God a part of our lives, we begin to grow in faith. This growth does not come by simply acquiring biblical facts, but when the Word of God has an intimate identification with the person of Jesus Christ (John 1:1, 14; 6:63; Revelation 19:13). The more the Word of God indwells and controls us, the more we are controlled by Jesus Christ. Then we have "the faith of Christ" (Galatians 2:16, 20). The more of his faith we get, the more we grow in our faith.

WE GROW IN FAITH THROUGH SEEKING THE LORD

The doctrine of "seeking" the Lord is not emphasized today. Maybe it is because we live in a day of "instant everything." We have instant food and instant replays. People think they can get instant knowledge. People want knowledge to be fed to them by television, seminars, or newspapers. As a result, we do not see many people seeking knowledge about God. But it is biblical to search for God. "When thou saidst, seek ye my face; my heart said unto thee, thy face, Lord, will I seek" (Psalm 27:8). Our faith will grow as we seek God, because when the soul is seeking God, it gets a clearer view of its own corruption. Specifically, the person comes to grips with the issues that keep him from growing in grace. As he seeks God, he identifies his egoism, and the lust of his flesh. Just as for salvation, you must get a man lost before you can get him saved, so for the Christian life, you must show a man the greatness of his sin before he realizes the greatness of the Savior.

Next, when a person seeks God, he searches out his own heart, looking for a better relationship with his Savior. He gets more than a theoretical understanding of God. He comes to know God on an experiential level. The person who is seeking God continually asks, "Is my all on the altar?" In the Old Testament, the priest laid the animal sacrifice on the altar for the saint. In the New Testament, the cross of Jesus Christ is our altar and we must make sure that every sin is forgiven. When we bring our sins to the cross, we are growing in faith.

WE GROW IN FAITH THROUGH CONSTANT CLEANSING BY THE BLOOD

God constantly cleanses the Christian through the blood of Calvary, "If we walk in the light, as he is in the light, . . . the blood of Jesus Christ his Son cleanseth us from all sin" (1 John 1:7). Daily cleansing makes possible continued fellowship in Jesus Christ. Our position in heaven is perfect, but on earth we may sin and destroy fellowship with God and other Christians. When this happens, we must recognize sin each time it occurs and confess it for cleansing and restoration to fellowship with God. Because "If we confess our sins, he is faithful and just to forgive us our sins, and to cleanse us from all unrighteousness" (1 John 1:9). So, every time we recognize sin in our lives and rid ourselves of its hindrance, we grow in faith.

Sometimes confession requires apologies and restitution. Not only must we deal with sin between us and God, we must deal with sin that hinders our fellowship with other Christians. Since confession of sin is a constant experience, so the Christian will constantly grow in his faith as he constantly relies upon the Lord.

WE GROW IN FAITH BY NOT TRUSTING SELF
One of the great mysteries in life is faith. It is difficult to tell who is exercising it, and who is kidding himself. When it comes to living by faith, some people actually experience communion with God day by day; they live by faith. Others deceive themselves, thinking they are living by faith, when they are simply feeding off the atmosphere of their church. As in self-hypnosis, they have convinced themselves that they have what others around them have. They have been deceived. In the future, these people will give up when they face a difficulty.

Those who have self-hypnotized faith are not hypocrites. They have heard the expression "let go and let God." To them, faith was a leap in the dark, not knowing what they were doing. Since they desire to have God's best, they leap for it. Out of desperation or a hope that lightning may strike, they continue the charade. They claim to have faith when they do not know what they are seeking. It is like the farmer who incorrectly said, "Faith is believing what you know ain't so."

Faith is never blind faith. At least it is not blind faith in God. God doesn't work through ignorance. Since faith is grounded in the Bible and is directed by the Holy Spirit, then our faith must be established on the facts of the Bible because faith will never go contrary to the nature of God or the principles by which God works. Therefore, we can never have blind faith in God or his Word. But there will be occasions when we will not understand our circumstances nor see the results that we seek. At that time it may seem we are exercising "blind faith." Paul described it, "We walk by faith not by sight" (2 Corinthians 5:7). But we shouldn't call it "blind faith," because that may mislead an unknowing Christian.

WE GROW IN FAITH THROUGH SURRENDER

The Christian must constantly surrender to the lordship of the Lord Jesus Christ. We do this once, when we are saved. As a result, our entire lives are dedicated to Jesus Christ. But also, there are subsequent times to surrender to Christ. We do this each time a crisis or problem arises in our lives. So every time we yield our lives to the Lord, we grow in grace.

Surrender is an unreserved yes to the standards of Jesus Christ. When we were first saved, the act of surrender was called *repentance*. After we were saved, the act of surrender is called *consecration, dedication,* or *yieldedness*. In this act, the Christian abandons both his sin and his allegiance to his flesh. In that act of surrender, he takes on the aims of the Lord Jesus Christ.

We are not talking about sinless perfection or total eradication. The act of surrender is simply allowing the Lord to be ruler of our lives. Paul made the appeal, "I beseech you therefore, brethren, by the mercies of God, that ye present your bodies a living sacrifice, holy, acceptable unto God, which is your reasonable service" (Romans 12:1).

Growing in faith means we are trusting God more every

day. We are trusting God for position, power, advancement, and even our possessions in life. When we surrender, we reexamine our motives in everything. We are not looking after the needs of our flesh. We are attempting to obey Jesus Christ.

Here it should be noted that the life of faith is not the life of asceticism, or the denial of self. Faith is not a negative denial of self, but a positive seeking to manifest the Lord Jesus Christ in every way. Therefore, it is possible for a person to work hard for a better salary, possessions, and influence when his motive is surrendered to God. It is possible to live by faith and be a successful businessman. If faith is looking at the Lord Jesus Christ, then no matter what a Christian does—get wealth or give up wealth—he looks to the Lord Jesus Christ in everything. Wealthy Abraham was one of the greatest examples of faith in the Bible. However, the Christian needs to be warned that earthly possessions easily blind one's sight. Shortly thereafter, possessions rather than the Word of God may become the road map for one's life journey.

But yielding to God is a difficult transaction. Yielding is also elusive, like quicksilver, because the heart is deceitful. We cannot trust our feelings or our inclinations. We can only trust the fact that we have put everything on the altar. Yielding is nothing more than making a commitment to Christ.

Many people want to diet and lose weight. They dream of losing weight, they talk of losing weight, and they buy special diet books on losing weight. Even though they have these desires, they do not lose weight because they never make a commitment. So those who lose weight are those who make a commitment to do what is necessary. In the same way, those who walk by faith are those who make a commitment to God.

There are many today who want to be holy. They read books about prayer, hear sermons about the Christian life, and attend Sunday school where classes are given about how to attain the deeper life. However, they cannot experience a life of faith because they have never made a commitment to walk by faith. The life of faith begins when a person yields the basic core of his life to Jesus Christ.

WE GROW IN FAITH BY NOT FIGHTING

Many years ago my little daughter was pleased with her progress in learning to swim. While vacationing in Canada, she swam out of a quiet pool into the rapid current. She screamed and fought the current. I could see sheer panic in her face but I knew she was in shallow water and was not in trouble. I jumped in the water and, grabbing her, forced her to stand on the hard rock bottom.

Many Christians respond like my daughter when faced with a problem that threatens their lives. They struggle to the point of exhaustion. They need to surrender and stop fighting the current. They need to stand on the rock bottom.

Jesus described this action, "If any man will come after me, let him deny himself" (Matthew 16:24). When a man surrenders, he stops struggling for self-advancement or self-protection. However, surrender does not mean he quits working. When faced with a problem he has to work all the harder. But he works with different motives. He applies the principles of God's Word and stops fighting the circumstances. He commits the problem to the Lord and no longer tries to solve the problem in his own way for his own purpose. He surrenders to God's principles and allows God's power to flow through him as he applies his solution.

WE GROW IN FAITH THROUGH CONSTANT COMMUNION

If we want growing faith, we must have constant communion with Jesus Christ. As we drive down the expressway, we can talk to Christ without closing our eyes. As we work in the kitchen, we can sense his presence without seeing him with our physical eyes. The life of faith is the life of communion with the resurrected Jesus Christ.

The path to communion with Christ is following the conditions of faith. We make a commitment to master the Word of God, through memorizing its concepts, meditating on its precepts, and obeying its laws. We commit ourselves to prayer, Christian service, and fellowship with other Christians.

WE GROW IN FAITH THROUGH HIS FAITH

The secret to the Christian life is not our faith, but the faith of Jesus Christ. "I am crucified with Christ: nevertheless I live; yet not I, but Christ liveth in me: and the life which I now live in the flesh I live by the faith of the Son of God, who loved me, and gave himself for me" (Galatians 2:20). We must learn to live by the faith of Jesus Christ. Because he is the Son of God, Jesus had the greatest faith known to man, and it is available to us.

Jesus said, "I always please the Father," hence he is our example to please the Father. We can have the faith of Jesus Christ when we allow him to indwell our lives and live his faith through us. Then our faith becomes his faith, and then we can learn the secret to overcome the world. John said, "This is the victory that overcometh the world, even our faith. Who is he that overcometh the world, but he that believeth that Jesus is the Son of God?" (1 John 5: 4, 5).

TEN
KEPT BY FAITH

*Now it is faith to believe that which you do not yet see;
and the reward of faith is to see that which you believe.*
St. Augustine

Perhaps we are not able to move mountains with our faith. We have said what we wanted but the answers did not come. Perhaps our faith is not complete. Our faith is not the kind the Bible describes as that which brings praise, honor, and glory to Jesus Christ. The path to effective faith is through trials.

Peter wrote, "The trial of your faith, being much more precious than of gold that perisheth, though it be tried with fire, might be found unto praise and honour and glory at the appearing of Jesus Christ" (1 Peter 1:7). Peter described it as faith tried with fire. When God is allowing us to suffer, the end result will be Say-It-Faith for then our faith will be as pure gold.

Once we are saved, our faith is nurtured in circumstances. God wants us to have faith in himself because that pleases and glorifies him. But faith is not something God can give to his subjects. It must come from our hearts that are governed by our free will. To develop our faith, God will sometimes maneuver us into a corner so that we creatures will look to the Creator. When we are put in such a situation, then we have opportunity to grow in faith.

When Hudson Taylor was faced with a problem, he prayed, he wept, he fasted, but only when he recognized God was the solution to his predicament could he find a solution. In that sense, personal faith grows out of problems or trials.

The Bible teaches that faith is contrary to the old nature and those who constantly follow the ways of the natural man cannot please God—they cannot walk by faith.

Trusting the ways of the old nature is putting trust in money, in the family, in a job, or in an organization to solve problems. But those who walk by faith put their trust in God.

When Jacob was coming back to meet his brother, Esau, he was terrified with the prospect of meeting an offended enemy. Jacob had stolen Esau's birthright. Because of his deceit and Esau's consequent anger, Jacob had fled. The night before Jacob met his brother, he met the angel of the Lord at the brook Jabbok. All night Jacob wrestled with God. When the morning dawned, the angel of the Lord demanded to be released. Jacob, in an act of frustration borne out of circumstances, announced, "I will not let thee go, except thou bless me" (Genesis 32:26). Even though Jacob was in trouble, he recognized that the solution to his problem came from God. While Jacob was a deceiver, he exercised faith and in that trust became Israel, the prince of God.

Faith recognizes the struggle between the flesh and the Spirit (Romans 8:5-8). Many want to become great men of faith but their lives are shallow and superficial. They want to walk with God, yet never experience God's presence. Even when they try to exercise faith, it seems to no avail. Why do some men have great faith and others little faith?

To get more faith, we must first look at Jesus Christ and

see him correctly. But, second, we must look within our hearts and see our sinful nature. Those who correctly understand their flesh, realize it will keep them from walking by faith. The flesh is in a civil war against the Spirit of God. The Bible says, "The flesh lusteth against the Spirit and are contrary one to the other" (Galatians 5:17). This means that the flesh, which is deceitful and desperately wicked will keep a man from walking by faith. Some Christians are blind to this problem.

The heart is so deceitful that it will deceive a Christian, making him think he is acceptable to God, when in fact he is walking by the flesh. Some preachers can spend all week preparing a sermon and then preach a powerless message on Sunday. They have not recognized that the flesh will keep them from communion with God, and without walking with God, they have no spiritual power. Therefore, when we recognize the temptation from our sinful nature, we are beginning to lay a foundation on which to walk by faith.

An old saint once said, "I did not know I had a temper until after I was saved." The gentleman went on to confess he had never lost his temper in his life. But after conversion he recognized he was in mortal struggle with Satan, who would keep him from being holy.

After we recognize the old nature, we must also realize that the new nature gives us power to please God. Paul stated, "I delight in the law of God after the inward man" (Romans 7:22). The new nature always wants to do the work of God. The saved man has counter forces working in his heart. He has temptations to do evil and desires to do good. His temptation comes from the old nature. "The evil which I would not, that I do" (Romans 7:19). The desire to do good comes from God, who gives us a new nature at conversion. The child of God wants to avoid sin. Paul describes it, "And that which I would not, that I do." Such a struggle is commonplace among those who want to walk by faith. When a saint wrestles by the Holy Spirit for righteousness and against the lust of the flesh, he is exercising faith.

But some Christians do not seem to have a problem with flesh. At least this seems to be their outward experience. Actually, when the lust of the flesh seems to go away, it does not go very far. As the country farmer said, "The old nature plays possum, meaning it goes to sleep and lets you think it will not bother you until it is ready to trap you." Therefore, the man of faith must always be alert to the snares of the devil.

Walking in the flesh is doing what we want to do, the way we want to do it, at the time we want to do it. And after all is said and done, self is the last idol to be conquered in the Christian's life.

When Eve ate the fruit, it was for self-knowledge. When David committed adultery it was for self-satisfaction. When Demas forsook the Lord, it was for self-love. Too often we blame the devil for our sin, when actually the source of our temptation is self. This does not deny the existence of Satan—it affirms his existence, for he uses the selfish nature to tempt us. Martin Luther once said, "I am more afraid of my own heart than I am of the Pope." In the same theme, Paul said, "O wretched man that I am, who shall deliver me . . . ?" (Romans 7:24).

Faith recognizes that God is the only source of victory. A pilot of a small-engine aircraft once approached a storm on the horizon. According to the flight controllers, he could not go to the left or to the right, and when he flew close to the earth, he found that he could not go under. Realizing the crisis, he pulled back on the controls and flew the plane above the storm, dangerously close to the oxygen level. Finally, he came out on top of the storm and was able to reach safety. In the same way the Christian faces catastrophic problems day after day. He is faced with sin, the devil and his old nature. When he cannot get around and cannot go under, the only victory is by going up to God himself.

Israel faced a crisis when she came to the Red Sea. There were mountains to both sides and a murderous Egyptian army closing in from the rear. Then God commanded, "Stand still and see the salvation of the Lord." Faith recognizes that the only victory we have is in the Lord himself.

God sends trials to drive us to himself. The next time there is a sickness in the family, we should realize God may be trying to teach us to trust him. The same thing happens when we lose a job, face a disappointment, or are strangled by despair. God is pulling us to himself.

Sometimes when we face a crisis, we want to lie down and quit—the route of despair. Other times when we face a crisis we want to retreat—the path of the coward. At other times when we face a crisis we feel we must do something quickly—the path of impetuousness. Other times we face the Red Sea, we try to walk on water—the route of presumptuousness. The only right response is turning to God who is able to give us victory.

We cannot have victory by reliance on our inner life. God does not use our flesh and make it work better. God does not polish up the flesh, nor does he give it a new direction. The flesh cannot please God. The only thing the flesh can do is drive us to God who gives us victory.

God does not take away the operations of the flesh. God gives us a new desire for righteousness that is placed alongside the old drive to sin. The flesh with its lust remains; it is a mighty engine. When self is controlling, the flesh is driven by the lower appetites of our souls and is fueled by Satan who rebels in the face of Almighty God. There is nothing in man to give him victory. We need not look within our hearts, there is no faith in the flesh. Victory comes by faith in Jesus Christ.

Our only victory is in the triumph of Jesus Christ. When Jesus Christ died, he was nailed to the cross to suffer vicariously for our sins. John the Baptist cried, "Behold the Lamb of God, which taketh away the sin of the world"

(John 1:29). But the death of Christ means more than an action that takes away the guilt of our sin. The death of Christ also added the righteousness of Christ to our account. Salvation has both a positive and negative side (2 Corinthians 5:21). "For he hath made him to be sin for us, who knew no sin; that we might be made the righteousness of God in him." This means that in death Christ took away our sin and gave us his righteousness.

Satan seemingly was victorious over Christ at the cross. Even the Scripture predicted an apparent victory by Satan over Jesus Christ, "thou shalt bruise his heel." This means that Satan shall seemingly inflict the death-wound on the Savior. But the promise goes on to say, "It shall bruise thy head" (Genesis 3:15), meaning Jesus Christ, the seed of the woman, shall have the ultimate victory over Satan.

Our victory is in Jesus Christ who is the victorious One, "Thanks be unto God, which always causeth us to triumph in Christ" (2 Corinthians 2:14).

Therefore, if we want victorious faith, it must be grounded in the victory of Jesus Christ over sin. This means the only way for us to get victory over sin is to apply the benefits of the death of Christ to our problem.

But our victory goes farther than identification with his death. It also identifies with his new life. The Bible teaches that in death there was life. "Therefore we are buried with him by baptism into death; that like as Christ was raised up from the dead by the glory of the Father, even so we also should walk in newness of life" (Romans 6:4). Our ability to walk in our new faith is based on the life that Jesus Christ gave us because of the resurrection.

Therefore, to walk in victorious faith over problems is to appropriate the benefits of Jesus Christ. After identifying with the crucified life, making sure our sins have been covered by his blood, we must go on to let the indwelling Son of God give us power over sin.

There is no victory without the blood of Jesus Christ, for "without shedding of blood is no remission" (Hebrews

9:22), and "without faith it is impossible to please him, for he that cometh to God must believe that he is, and that he is a rewarder of them that diligently seek him" (Hebrews 11:6). We get an abundant victory over sin through the crucified life. Jesus announced, "I am come that they might have life, and that they might have it more abundantly" (John 10:10). The basis of life was his death, mentioned in the next verse, "I am the good shepherd; the good shepherd giveth his life for the sheep" (John 10:11).

When Israel came to the Promised Land, the people could not enter into their promise because of the overflowing Jordan River. It was spring, and the rains had flooded the Jordan Valley. God told Israel to wait three days (Joshua 1:11), symbolic of the three days' death experience of Jesus Christ. Then after three days, God commanded the priests to take the ark of the covenant, symbolic of the presence of God, and enter into the Jordan. The command was not to stop at the banks of the Jordan, but to walk into the Jordan with the presence of God. As the priests' feet touched the water, the flood rolled back and became dry sand under the feet of all Israel. Their victory over the obstacle of the Jordan River was symbolic of the death of Christ. Just so, we get our victory through the death of Jesus Christ.

Paul explained, "If one died for all, then were all dead: And that he died for all, that they which live should not henceforth live unto themselves, but unto him which died for them, and rose again" (2 Corinthians 5:14, 15).

Our victory is in Christ's victory. We cannot change our lives. Only Jesus Christ can change our motives and destinies. The Bible says, "That which is crooked cannot be made straight" (Ecclesiastes 1:15). So the man who is a drunkard cannot change his nature, nor can a couple who bicker and fight get supernatural love. Victory over their problems comes from Jesus Christ. Our only hope to live a peaceable life is to have him who is our peace.

An old Scottish interpretation of Psalm 96:10 goes, "Say unto the people, the Lord reigneth from the tree." So Jesus Christ can reign in our hearts because of Calvary. Our victory is in that terrible death on the tree (Galatians 3:13).

Therefore, the Christian, like Israel, must cross the Jordan. And as the Christian crosses his obstacles, he will possess the Promised Land. God has promised victory for our lives if we will only claim it. However, we cannot possess our Promised Land until we are possessed by the Savior.

ELEVEN
OVERCOMING THE FACTORS THAT DESTROY FAITH

"Faith," then is first the hand of the soul which "lays hold of" the contents of God's promises; second, it is the eye of the soul which looks out toward and represents them clearly and convincingly to us. Arthur Pink

Our Christian lives begin with saving faith and end with Say-It-Faith. Our faith guides us every step toward maturity. Many factors crush a person's faith before he arrives at the place where he can move mountains by the word of faith.

Peter wrote, "Giving all diligence, add to your faith virtue; and to virtue knowledge; and to knowledge temperance; and to temperance patience; and to patience godliness; and to godliness brotherly kindness; and to brotherly kindness charity. For if these things be in you, and abound, they make you that you shall neither be barren nor unfruitful in the knowledge of our Lord Jesus Christ" (2 Peter 1:5-8).

When everyone arrived at Sunday school at the First Baptist Church of West Hollywood, Florida, they saw a large sign they did not understand, "I Love 5,000." At the entrance to the church, hostesses pinned a card on each pupil that also stated, "I Love 5,000." During the assembly, Pastor Verle Ackerman announced a goal to the congregation of reaching 5,000 in Sunday school. At the time attendance averaged 2,500, but Pastor Ackerman felt that "by faith" they should take a goal of doubling the attendance. The goal of 5,000 people was a challenge to every person to bring someone to Sunday school.

After Ackerman announced the goal, he asked everyone to unpin the card on his lapel and write across the back, "I will pray twenty-one times for 5,000 people to attend Sunday school." The pastor challenged the people to pray for the goal every time they ate one of the twenty-one meals during the coming week. As a result of the pastor's faith, over 5,300 attended Sunday school. Pastor Ackerman had expressed Say-It-Faith and all who shared in his faith were strengthened.

But we must realize that not everyone who claims to exercise Say-It-Faith actually moves mountains. Some people have set an attendance goal but have missed it. Other people have prayed for money by faith and the finances did not come in. There are hindrances to faith and if we understand these obstacles, we can trust God more.

Faith is not the same as the power of positive thinking. The secret of positive thinking is to talk oneself into a frame of mind so that he can accomplish what he desires. As good as positive thinking is, it is not faith. To some, the power of positive thinking is nothing more than "psyching oneself up" to make a sale or to do one's best in a sport. If our faith is not grounded on Bible faith, we cannot expect God to work in us or through us. The secret of faith is belief in God. Jesus said, "When ye pray, believe that ye receive them, and ye shall have them" (Mark 11:24).

THE JACOB FACTOR
No matter how hard we believe, we do not have New Testament faith if we believe a lie. When Jacob was an old

man, he was told by his ten sons that Joseph, the son to whom he had given the coat of many colors, had been killed by an animal. As the ten sons stood before Joseph, they had in their hands the coat of many colors, covered with blood. The outward circumstances pointed to Joseph's death and Jacob believed it. He mourned for twenty years, believing a lie.

The Jacob factor will keep our faith from growing. If we put our faith in baptism to save us, we have been told a lie. We do not have New Testament faith nor can we call God our heavenly Father. Perhaps we have put our human faith in a minister, and he has disappointed us. Some preachers have drifted into sin. Others have denied the faith. Perhaps someone has hurt our faith, because he was living a lie. Even though we "believe with all our hearts," God cannot honor our faith if the object of our faith is a lie.

After twenty years Jacob was told that his son Joseph was alive. At first Jacob could not believe it, "and Jacob's heart fainted, for he believed them not" (Genesis 45:26). It is a terrible thing not to be able to believe what is said. It is terrible to have a skeptical heart. But then Jacob's sons "told him all the words of Joseph, which he had said unto them: and when he saw the wagons which Joseph had sent to carry him, the spirit of Jacob their father revived" (Genesis 45:27). Then Jacob said, "It is enough; Joseph my son is yet alive" (Genesis 45:28).

The Jacob factor is always a problem. If we trust someone's interpretation of the Bible and he is wrong, we cannot have New Testament faith. We cannot trust the interpretation of men, but we can trust the Word of God. Once again, our faith must be grounded upon the absolute truth of the Word of God but we must make sure we have correctly interpreted the Word of God.

Later, the entire nation of Israel was deceived by the Jacob factor. When the twelve spies went into the Promised Land, they were commissioned to bring back a report. Their message became the basis on which the nation refused to enter the Promised Land. The spies brought back the message that the Promised Land was flowing with milk and honey, but there were great walled cities. Finally the spies described Israel as "grasshoppers," and the inhabitants of the land as "giants." The fear of the spies became the fear of Israel. Israel could not believe God and refused to enter the Promised Land. They drew back in unbelief. As a result, every person over twenty years of age died in the wilderness. Why? Because they believed a lie. Their punishment was not because of their lack of sincerity. Their punishment was because they placed their trust in the wrong report. Sometimes a committee will say to the church, "We do not have enough money" and the church draws back in unbelief. On another occasion, the pastor has said, "No one is coming to soul-winning visitation, so let's cancel it." When the people believed the pastor, they did not aggressively go out to win souls and their spiritual life began to die.

THE PHILIP FACTOR
Approximately 5,000 men plus women and children had been listening to Jesus preach all day. Since they were hungry, Jesus wanted to feed them. The Master turned to Philip and said, "Whence shall we buy bread, that these may eat?" (John 6:5). This seems like an innocent question but the Bible goes on to say, "This he said to prove him [Philip] for he himself knew what he would do" (John 6:6). Jesus knew he was going to perform a miracle to feed the 5,000 people, but he was testing Philip to see if he had faith. After all, Philip had seen Jesus give sight to the blind and heal the lame.

Jesus expected Philip to answer in faith. But Philip analyzed the situation and gave facts to Jesus. "Two hundred penny worth of bread is not sufficient for them, that every one of them may take a little" (John 6:7). In essence, Philip said, "If we have approximately ninety-six cents for each person, we could only feed them a little bit." When a person is guilty of the Philip factor he is relying on his rational ability rather than on the Word of Christ.

A person cannot accept the statements of Jesus Christ if his mind rejects the weight of evidence for them. Rationalism sometimes gets in the way of faith. The Philip factor blocks faith as trash blocks the fuel line in a car. True New Testament faith must be our subjective trust in those things that we perceive to be true. But our faith is more than accepting those things that appear to be true. They must in reality be the truth.

When our minds accept a thing as true, they will automatically go on regarding that thing as true until something changes our minds. So if a person believes there are mistakes in the Bible, he will go on rejecting Jesus Christ until someone convinces him that the Bible is consistent and perfect without error.

Also, the mind will go on thinking in a certain pattern, just as traffic continues down the one-way street, unless something interrupts the flow of thought. If we have always relied on our reason, it is hard to accept anything by faith.

A boy who could not learn to swim kept viewing the old swimming hole. He knew rationally that heavy objects sink in water. He had seen people jump into the water and sink, but at the same time he knew that by the act of swimming, other boys could move through the water. He knew these things but he had to act, to get in and swim, to change his thinking. He had to go beyond rationalism to volition.

The potential faith of many is destroyed by the Philip factor. Instead of leading a person to Christ through the Bible plan of salvation, some want to reason with them so that the unconverted accepts Christianity like he learns a mathematical formula. Some churches cannot go forward because of the Philip factor. Someone figures out mathematically that a revival cannot pay for itself, or the church cannot afford to take on the support of extra missionaries. As a result the church does not step out by faith.

There is a battle between faith and the mind. New Testament faith marches to the tune of the Bible. The human mind follows a different drum beat, limited by reason.

THE PETER FACTOR

Peter had many qualities. Perhaps he was best known as an impetuous, spontaneous, and enthusiastic "water walker." When Jesus came to the disciples in the storm at night, they cried out for fear. These seasoned fishermen were afraid of drowning. When Jesus invited, "Come," Peter was the only one to jump out of the boat and walk on water. In contrast, there were eleven "boat sitters" who did not respond to the command of Jesus Christ.

The Peter factor is often a blind leap into the dark. On another occasion, Peter grabbed the sword and sliced off the ear of Malcus, the temple servant, who came with the soldiers to arrest Jesus Christ. What Peter did in walking on the water and defending the Lord was done hastily and sincerely. Peter denied the old adage, "Look before you leap."

Faith is not a blind leap in the dark; faith is a "leap into the light." To walk by faith we must always step into the light of the Word of God.

Some students have rushed off to Bible college, trusting God for finances. The problem is that these students have left debts at home that needed to be paid. They came to Bible college and incurred more debts which also needed to be paid. I have seen some of these students make a shipwreck of their lives. Ultimately, they could not return to school because of their debts to the college. Their faith was not wrong. They were impetuous in disobeying the biblical principle about paying one's debts. Others were mistaken in what they thought was the call of God to go into full-time Christian service.

Some pastors have led their churches into an extensive bond program only later to be forced to file bankruptcy. The resulting financial problems became an embarrassment to the church and to the cause of Jesus Christ.

The cause of the Peter factor comes when a person bases his faith on a verse taken out of context. A young boy in New York read the Scriptures, "Go south" and he went to a Bible college in South Carolina. God blessed his life because he had a yielded spirit; however, one might question whether his faith was based on a correct interpretation of Scripture or something else. We must be careful not to take the commands of Scripture out of context. When God told Moses to send the ark of the covenant into the swollen Jordan River, God also promised to roll back the flood waters. We cannot expect to command flooding rivers to roll back unless God tells us he will do it, no matter how much faith we have. The historical principles of Scripture, however, can be applied today. We can go to the Bible and apply the biblical principles we find—this is faith. Since biblical principles are eternal, they apply to the twentieth century as well as to the first century. Therefore, our faith will grow when it is based on the principles of the Word of God. God does not expect us to walk on water as Peter, but God does expect us to be faithful witnesses as he was.

THE THOMAS FACTOR

Many Christians have stumbled in their faith because they wanted God to do something special for them. Some have asked God for special signs so their faith could grow. Since the basis of faith is the Word of God, God speaks through his Word, not in special signs. When the disciples told Thomas they had seen the Lord, he said, "Except I shall see in his hands the print of the nails, and put my finger into the print of the nails, and thrust my hand into his side, I will not believe" (John 20:25). It is a terrible thing to say, "I will not believe." But that is the danger of the Thomas factor.

Today, people still want an experience or a sign. Dr. W. A. Criswell, pastor of First Baptist Church of Dallas, Texas, talked about hearing testimonies as a young lad in brush-arbor meetings. He heard a deacon say, "God sent a ball of fire out of heaven that struck my soul." The man went on to claim, "I fell on my knees and cried out to God." Young Criswell heard that testimony and tried to duplicate the experience. The deacon concluded, "I prayed through until I got peace." Many people want to thrust their hands into Jesus' side before they believe. The Thomas factor is nothing more than demanding empirical evidence for faith.

When the Lord appeared to his disciples eight days later, he singled out Thomas for an act of faith. He said, "Reach hither thy hand, and thrust it into my side: and be not faithless, but believing" (John 20:27). But Thomas did not, as far as we can tell, actually put his hand into the side of the Lord, nor did he stick his finger into the wounds in the Lord's hands. He fell at his feet and cried out, "My Lord and my God" (20:28).

Those who ask Jesus Christ for a sign don't usually get it. Those who ask for a ball of fire, probably will never experience it. God wants people to base their faith on the Word of God. Jesus told Thomas, "Because thou hast seen me, thou hast believed" (John 20:29), but then Jesus commended others who believed without signs. "Blessed are they that have not seen, and yet have believed" (John 20:29).

Some who have Thomas faith begin with sincerity. They know the difficulty in their hearts of trusting God. Since faith is coupled with sincerity, we must recognize unbelief in our hearts before we can build sincere faith. This is the same principle of the contractor digging away soft dirt so that he may pour the foundation upon a solid rock. Thomas faith is belief that begins with unbelief. When we look in our hearts and see unbelief, we should not despair, but we should be honest and confess it, and go immediately to the Word of God. If we are honest to recognize our unbelief but at the same time, in honesty, recognize our belief, we have no hypocrisy in our hearts. We are building our faith because we are absolutely sincere in our hearts.

The Thomas factor also involves fear. Many people will not express Say-It-Faith because they are afraid that they will be wrong. Perhaps they were wrong before and lost their self-confidence. But Say-It-Faith is not confidence in self; it is confidence in God. However, we cannot deny that fear has weakened the faith of many Christians. Some will not ask their friends to pray for them, because they are afraid that God might not answer them.

Another reflection of the Thomas factor is people who have trouble with ego. They are reluctant to do anything for themselves because they feel little or no self-acceptance. As a result they will not act in faith. People who cannot trust themselves cannot trust God. Their lack of self-confidence destroys their faith in God, not because the one helps the other, but these people have no confidence in anything at all.

THE ANDREW FACTOR

One of the greatest characteristics of Andrew was that he began with the material close at hand. When Jesus and Philip were discussing how much money was necessary to feed 5,000 men, Andrew said, "There is a lad here, which hath five barley loaves, and two small fishes" (John 6:9). Andrew did not try to figure out where to find a delicatessen that was open, nor did he consider wholesale grocery suppliers. He looked to the answer closest at hand, the lunch of a small boy. In one sense Andrew should be commended for suggesting the small boy could help, but he did not exercise faith. Andrew also said when he saw the fish and bread, "But what are they among so many?" (John 6:9). The Andrew factor keeps people from taking the big view, and sometimes the eternal view. However, faith always begins where it finds the man, and lifts him to God. We should not seek for faith that is far away, nor for faith in difficult places. We should grow our faith where it is planted.

Some people will always have small faith because they always look for the closest solution. When Moses told God that he was unable to serve him, God asked him what he had in his hand. It was nothing but a rod (Exodus 4:2), but eventually God used the rod to divide the Red Sea. The rod was also used to bring water from the rock.

Faith is like a headlight of a car; it does not illuminate at once the entire ten miles of a trip. The headlight only illumines several hundred feet in advance. When the car has traveled that few hundred feet, the next several hundred feet light up. Those who live by faith usually can see only one day at a time, and sometimes one week or one month at a time. However, as we walk in faith, God leads us on many ten-mile journeys.

If we think that our faith is small, we should remember the Andrew factor and begin where we are and look at the faith we have.

OVERCOMING OBSTACLES TO FAITH
We have examined several obstacles that will either destroy our faith in Jesus Christ or keep it from growing. We should remember the following principles when our faith gets in trouble.

First, we are human, and humans change. One day we

love God deeply, while the next day our emotions can embitter us. This does not mean that our relationship to God has changed. It means only that sin has gained control of our lives or has blinded our perception of God. If we recognize that we change, we remember that the problem is not with God but with us.

The second step is that we must ground our faith on the facts of the Bible. Just because our love fluctuates does not mean that our faith is fickle.

Third, we should make sure our faith goes beyond our rational understanding of the will of God. We must never let our faith be grounded in our ability to perceive God, but take everything God has said in his Word. Remember, even our understanding can change. What we do not understand about God today may be plain next week. When we go out in the morning we may perceive that it is going to rain, so we take an umbrella to work. However, what we thought was rain was simply ground fog. The sun burns away the mist and the day is beautiful. We must not let the fog of unbelief cloud our perception of the Bible. We must look for what God has placed in the Bible and accept it as his will.

Fourth, we must be careful of the influence of circumstances on our lives. For instance, a person thinks that his mother is dying of cancer. Because of this he questions God. All the while, his mother has only a small cyst, not a cancer. When we put our eyes on circumstances, our faith questions God, when it should have trusted him.

But even if a person's mother has cancer, he should not let the circumstances control his faith. Faith should help a person to control his circumstances.

Fifth, our faith needs daily nurture. Like the flowers that wither without water, and the body that dies without food, our faith will grow weaker (Romans 4:18-20) if it is not nurtured through Bible study, prayer, and Christian obedience. As the Christian applies the Word of God to his life, he is reminded of what he believes and how his faith should grow.

No faith automatically remains alive in the soul. Some people have lost their faith (subjective faith) because they have fed it sin. This does not mean that they have lost their salvation. They have lost their fellowship with God. But when they lose their subjective faith, they live empty lives.

Sixth, we should accept the unbelief we find in our hearts, rather than condemning ourselves. Because we have a sin nature, we cannot have perfect faith. Also, our minds are finite. We do not know everything, hence we cannot have explicit faith in God. Just as a Christian becomes humble by realizing his lack of humility, so a Christian builds up his faith by realizing his unbelief.

When we see our need, we are motivated to build up our faith. No one knows the evil in his heart until he tries to serve God with all his being, so no one experiences true biblical faith until he has attempted to "trust in the Lord with all thine heart" (Proverbs 3:5). As we stand on the riverbank and view the tide, we never know the strength of the current until we attempt to swim the stream. A man who never tries to live for God has never experienced his sinful nature.

Seventh, we must recognize the conditional nature of life. Rather than our saying by faith, I know that I am to move to a certain city, we should say, "If it is the will of God." James wrote: "Go to now, ye that say, To day or to morrow we will go into such a city, and continue there a year, and buy and sell, and get gain: Whereas you know not what shall be on the morrow" (James 4:13, 14). No one knows how long he will live, nor what will befall him. James tells us, "For that ye ought to say, if the Lord will, we shall live, and do this, or that" (James 4:15).

CONCLUSION

God has given many qualities to man, as demonstrated in his giving the fruit of the Spirit and the gifts of the Spirit. These qualities are given primarily to help us relate to ourselves, to other Christians, or to our service for God. But faith is a quality that has a different dimension. It is the one quality that moves God. As a matter of fact, faith pleases God and faith, correctly exercised, results in God moving the mountains that face us. Therefore, we seem to need greater faith to accomplish greater works (John 14:12).

Dr. Howard Hendricks of Dallas Theological Seminary once preached a sermon that balanced this perspective. He challenged the audience: "Don't seek greater faith," explaining that if we do, we have then focused on man and not on God. Dr. Hendricks pointed us to the source of faith. "We don't need greater faith—we need a greater understanding of God in our lives."

That is right! When we have a greater vision of the person of God, and have a greater understanding of his plan in our lives, and we respond with greater dedication and zeal, then we have Say-It-Faith that can move mountains.

FOOTNOTES

CHAPTER 5

1 Roland Bainton, *Here I Stand* (Nashville: Abingdon Press, 1956), p. 65.
2 Martin Luther, *A Commentary on St. Paul's Epistle to the Galatians* (Westwood, NJ: Fleming H. Revell Company, First printed in 1575. No date given for recent printing), p. 12.
3 *Ibid.*
4 Bainton, *op. cit.,* p. 13.

CHAPTER 6

1 Richard N. Longenecker, *Paul, Apostle of Liberty* (Grand Rapids: Baker Book House, 1964, reprint, 1976). p. 149.
2 T. F. Torrance, "One Aspect of the Biblical Conception of Faith," *The Expository Times*, Vol. LXVIII, No. 4 (Jan., 1957, pp. 11-14).

BIBLIOGRAPHY

Bavinck, J. H. *Faith and Its Difficulties*. Grand Rapids: Wm. B. Eerdmans Publishing Co., 1959.
Binstock, Lewis. *The Power of Faith*. New York: Prentice-Hall Inc., 1952.
Buber, Martin. *Two Types of Faith*. New York: Harper and Brothers, 1951.
Finleyson, Spurgeon, Moody, Aitken, McLaren. *What is Faith?* Chicago: The Bible Institute Colportage Association, 1924.
Grenfell, Wilfred T. *A Man's Faith*. Boston: The Pilgrim Press, 1926.
Grubb, Norman. *The Law of Faith*. Christian Literature Crusade, 1947.
Machen, J. Gresham. *What Is Faith?* Grand Rapids: Wm. B. Eerdmans Publishing Co., 1925.
McKay, Donald J. *Unfeigned Faith*. Chicago: The Bible Institute Colportage Association, 1940.
Mundell, George H. *The Pathway of Faith*. Philadelphia: Self Published, 1951.
Murray, Andrew. *Why Do You Not Believe?* New York: Hurst & Co., 1894.
Orr, J. Edwin. *Faith That Makes Sense*. Valley Forge: Judson Press, 1960.
Rice, G. Christian. *Faith; Valid or Vain?* Lincoln: Back to the Bible, 1978.
Wilkes, Paget. *Dynamics of Faith*. London, England: Oliphants Ltd., 1925.